saturday kitchen
at home

saturday kitchen
at home

Over 140 recipes from 50 of your favourite chefs

BBC
BOOKS

Amanda Ross, Executive Producer of *Saturday Kitchen Live* who devised and co-edited this book would like to thank the following for their considerable efforts:

Anna Ratcliffe for keeping the chefs happy by enjoying every dish, *and* perfect proofing; Series Producer James Winter for his dedication to the show; Producer Andy Clarke for his creatively "camp" take on wine; the production team, Emma Welch, Chris Worthington, Dave Mynard, Elissa Standen, Will Learmonth, Matt, Jessica and Roxanne; Simon Ross for the format and devising the legendary omelette challenge; Janet Brinkworth and Michaela Bowles for food preparation; all our celebrity guests and the celebrity booking team, Charlotte Johnstone and Jonathan Perry; James and Tom for the VTs, Silvana Job for keeping order, Director Dino Charalambous; and the rest of the amazing happy crew, Jeremy, Naomi, Martin, Kev, Dave, Rob, Tom, Phil, Toby, Gary, Mitch, Murray, Neil, Viv, Lorraine, Pauly, Sean, Cal, Mel, Loulou, Sue, Steve, Nick, Dom, Jez, Ross, Ben, Nikki, Guy, Jim, the Barneys, and Geri who make getting up at 5am a happy thing to do on a Saturday morning; our BBC Executives – Liam Keelan, Carla-Maria Lawson and Gerard Melling; and of course, most of all, James Martin, and all the amazing chefs and wonderful wine experts – it's an amazing privilege and an even greater pleasure working with you all!

This book is published to accompany the television series produced by Cactus TV entitled *Saturday Kitchen Live*, broadcast on BBC1.

10 9 8 7 6 5 4 3 2 1

Published in 2010 by BBC Books, an imprint of Ebury Publishing. A Random House Group Company

Copyright © Cactus TV 2010
Photography © Kate Whitaker 2010
Design © Woodlands Books Ltd 2010

Cactus TV has asserted the right to be identified as the author of this Work in accordance with the Copyright, Designs and Patents Act 1988

The Random House Group Limited Reg. No. 954009

Addresses for companies within the Random House Group can be found at www.randomhouse.co.uk

A CIP catalogue record for this book is available from the British Library.

ISBN 978 1 846 07884 2

The Random House Group Limited supports the Forest Stewardship Council (FSC), the leading international forest certification organisation. All our titles that are printed on Greenpeace approved FSC certified paper carry the FSC logo. Our paper procurement policy can be found at www.rbooks.co.uk/environment

Mixed Sources
Product group from well-managed forests and other controlled sources
www.fsc.org Cert no. SGS-COC-005091
© 1996 Forest Stewardship Council

Contents

Introduction

The kitchen is the most important room in the house. Most people start and end every day there. It can be the engine-room that fuels a growing family, it can provide the ammunition and location for a romantic rendezvous, or it can just be a quiet place to knock up a simple supper. Whatever you use your kitchen for, most of them have the same basic things – a fridge, a cooker, some pots and pans and, most importantly, someone to do the cooking: the chef.

The *Saturday Kitchen Live* team are lucky to be able to call on the services of the very best chefs in the world to cook at our hobs. Well over 100 different chefs have passed through our studio on a Saturday morning. We have showcased the talents of some huge names in the food world, such as Michel Roux and Antonio Carluccio, as well as introducing and championing new faces like Adam Byatt and Fernando Stovell. All of them have a passion and a love of cooking that it's been our very great pleasure to share with you each weekend.

The chef's table guests are often surprised at how much preparation goes into making the show each week. The relaxed atmosphere in the studio and the chefs' accomplished performances often belie the careful planning that takes place well before anyone arrives on the day.

Dishes are chosen to illustrate a wide range of techniques and ingredients throughout the cooking process. We need to ensure that the viewers are getting a varied menu, as well as achievable recipes that look interesting on the plate. As important as the forward planning are the loyal and dedicated team behind the scenes who help prepare and cook, testing the recipes and getting everything ready so that the chefs can do a smooth live demonstration. Some chefs who are new to the show need help adapting their recipes to something we can understand in just eight minutes. We couldn't do this show without the many willing hands that get stuck into the mountains of washing up and help clear the set between, and during, each recipe!

By Friday of each week the scripts are ready, the wines have been chosen and filmed on location with our experts, and all the insert films have been edited. The Saturday of the live show begins early. The foodie team have to start arriving at the studio around 5 a.m. – fine in summer, but less fun in the dark of winter. The home economists begin the painstaking preparation of the cooking ingredients, after the obligatory bacon buttie of course. Talking of bacon sandwiches, and we often do, the cameramen who work on the show arrive next, the smell of the bacon drawing them in like moths to a flame. The production team are already buzzing around, finalising details and briefing guests.

Television programmes have many unsung heroes; those names you see flying by at the end of the show all have important roles. Each and every person who fixes a light, mends a microphone, sharpens a knife, works a camera, times a recipe, cleans a fridge or works the autocue is an integral part of the show. Without any one of them the jigsaw of the show doesn't fit together. It's a very low-budget production, so everyone needs to muck in to make that work and, as a result, there is a strong team spirit on *Saturday Kitchen Live* and a real sense of excitement about each programme. We really do have fun making the show, and that comes across on TV.

People often ask what the secret of the show's popularity is, and the short answer is that it's a mixture of many factors. Some people like seeing new chefs, some like the opportunity to experience Michelin-starred cooking at home, and the celebrity food choices are always revealing. The BBC archive shows are popular – Rick Stein has appeared in every episode we've made, and is the only chef to have done so. It is also great to look back at the amazing, groundbreaking work of the late, great Keith Floyd. However, the *Saturday Kitchen* team have one overriding philosophy: the food is the star. This ethos goes right through the team, from James Martin in front of the camera to the very last washer-upper. We all love the food – yes, we love eating it but we also love the theatre of making the food look interesting, and the sharing nature of the cooking process, and we think this passion for food is the key to *Saturday Kitchen Live*'s success.

James has been the brilliant host of the show since he took over in June 2006, and has been instrumental in making *Saturday Kitchen Live* compulsive viewing every weekend. We usually have around two and a half million of you joining us on our food adventure each week, around 30 per cent of everyone who's watching TV at that time. James has cooked over 400 of his own dishes on the show, and helped chop, peel and mix for hundreds more.

The chefs featured in this book represent some of the best in the world – we've been proud to work with them on the programme and are delighted to be able to share their work with you. All these terrific chefs' recipes have had a TV trial, and now you can easily recreate them in your own home – more than 140 recipes from 50 brilliant chefs.

Enjoy!

Saturday Kitchen cook's notes

All the recipes in this book can be cooked at home the same way they are cooked by the chefs in the studio kitchen – you don't need fancy implements, multiple ovens or five pairs of hands. However, we do suggest that you read through each recipe completely before starting a dish. As the recipes were originally designed by chefs who are used to cooking in busy restaurant kitchens, some require different components of a dish to be cooked simultaneously. Prepare the ingredients as listed and check through the whole method before you start to cook.

Oven temperatures

We use fan-assisted Fahrenheit ovens on the show. If you are cooking with a conventional oven (without fan assistance), follow the temperature guidelines in this book but increase the cooking time by about 10 minutes. Timings will vary between ovens, so make sure food is piping hot and meat is cooked through before serving.

Deep-fat frying

Be careful when cooking with hot oil. Follow the manufacturer's instructions for how to heat and cook with deep-fat fryers. Always use vegetable or sunflower oil for deep-fat frying.

Cookware

On the show, we use ovenproof pans and flameproof baking dishes, which can be used on the hob as well as in the oven. Most of the recipes in this book don't require you to use ovenproof or flameproof pots and pans, but there are a couple that do. We find they make the cooking process easier and save on washing up!

Eggs / Butter

All eggs are medium and butter is unsalted unless otherwise stated. Pregnant women, elderly people, babies and toddlers, and anyone who is unwell should avoid eating raw and partially cooked eggs.

Ethically sourced ingredients

Where possible, we use unrefined sugar, free-range organic chicken and eggs, humanely reared meat and sustainably caught fish and seafood from local suppliers. Particularly for wild game, make sure you go to a reputable supplier and ask your butcher where they source their meat. For veal recipes, look for rosé veal produced in the UK and bearing the Freedom Food label, which the RSPCA have recognised as high-welfare veal.

Wine

Where a wine was recommended to complement a particular recipe by our wine experts on the show, we have included the name in this book along with any comments on the wine so that you can try the combination at home.

Where to find the more unusual ingredients

The majority of the ingredients used in this book can be bought from supermarkets and greengrocers. Most supermarket chains now stock a wide range of more unusual ingredients but you might need to shop around as one supermarket may not stock them all. For the few ingredients that are a little harder to track down, below is a list of online mail order suppliers you might find helpful.

Japanese ingredients

Shiso / White miso paste / Mizuna leaves (also known as Japanese mustard) / Japanese breadcrumbs (Panko) / Yukari seasoning / Yaki niku barbecue sauce / Ao nori (edible seaweed) / Ume shu plums in plum wine
Try www.japancentre.com or www.mountfuji.co.uk, which are one-stop shops for all things Japanese.

Western European ingredients

Wild mushrooms, such as morels, mousserons, girolles, pied bleu, pied de mouton, chanterelles, trompettes and ceps / Cobnuts (a type of hazelnut) / Banana shallots / Batavia lettuce / Winter truffles / Micro cress (such as radish red stem cress, red mustard cress, basil green cress, peashoot cress, red chard cress, broccoli cress and celery leaf cress) / Micro greens (including basil, celery leaf, chervil, chives, coriander, Greek cress, kale, rocket and watercress) / Smoked sea salt / Borage shoots / Bull's blood leaves / Medlars
When in season, you should be able to find all these ingredients at a good local greengrocer or deli and in some larger supermarkets. Rock samphire can be found at good local fishmongers. Otherwise try online suppliers London Fine Foods Group at www.efoodies.co.uk or www.foodswild.com.

Mediterranean and Middle Eastern ingredients

Kadaifi pastry (also called Kataifi and Kadayif) / Fregola (semolina-based beads of pasta) / Sumac powder
Try www.turkishsupermarket.co.uk or www.melburyandappleton.co.uk.

Central and Far East Asian ingredients

Dried mango powder / Sichuan/Szechuan peppercorns / Black sesame seeds / Star fruit / Ming noodles / Ginger and garlic paste / Tamarind paste / Ghee (clarified butter) / Rock chives / Wonton skins/spring roll wrappers / Mooli radish (Daikon) / Thai basil leaves
Try www.theasiancookshop.co.uk, www.nacto-online.com and www.enticefoods.com for a good range of Thai, Chinese and Indian ingredients.

Caribbean ingredients

Ground pimento seeds / Chipotle chilli ketchup
Try www.thespiceshop.co.uk for pimento seeds and www.coolchile.co.uk or www.southdevonchillifarm.co.uk for chipotle chilli ketchup.

Chefs gallery

Rachel Allen

Jason Atherton

Galton
Blackiston

Raymond Blanc

Martin Blunos

Adam Byatt

Michael Caines

John Campbell

Antonio
Carluccio

Sam Clark

Gennaro
Contaldo

Richard Corrigan

Arthur
Potts Dawson

Matthew Fort

Daniel Galmiche

Bill Granger

Sophie Grigson

Stuart Gillies

Donna Hay

Mark Hix

Ken Hom

Madhur Jaffrey

Lawrence Keogh

Si King

Tom Kitchin

Atul Kochhar

Prue Leith

James Martin

Dave Myers

Nick Nairn

Glynn Purnell

Tana Ramsay

Theo Randall

Paul Rankin

Sarah Raven

Michel Roux

Silvena Rowe

Mark Sargeant

Vivek Singh

Rick Stein

Fernando Stovell

Jun Tanaka

James Tanner

Matt Tebbutt

Cyrus Todiwala

John Torode

Marcus Wareing

Nic Watt

Bryn Williams

Patrick Williams

James Martin
Serrano-wrapped rabbit with chicory and orange salad

Theo Randall
Spatchcock pigeon roasted on bruschetta with cavolo nero, pancetta and porcini mushrooms

Si King
Spiced roasted guinea fowl served with a coconut and cucumber salad

Jun Tanaka
Smoked pigeon salad with beetroot, apples and walnuts

Nick Nairn
Warm mallard salad with puy lentils and crispy parsnips

Matt Tebbutt
Spiced marinated rabbit with herbed couscous and pine nuts

Vivek Singh
Peanut and dried mango crusted partridge with a curry leaf and tomato quinoa

Antonio Carluccio
Fillet of venison and wild mushroom sauce

James Martin
Breaded pheasant breast with beetroot purée and marinated beetroot

Marcus Wareing
Roasted quail with watermelon, spring onion fondue, cobnuts and quail vinaigrette

Tom Kitchin
Roast teal, purple sprouting broccoli and salsify

Lawrence Keogh
Roast pheasant with sherry glazed parsnips and chestnuts

Si King
Loin of venison with a blackberry and sloe gin glaze served with clapshot rösti and parsnip crisps

Atul Kochhar
Spiced venison with pear chutney and sweet spicy parsnip

James Martin
Roasted partridge with creamed Brussels sprouts and chestnuts

James Martin
Wild boar pie with roast parsnips

Game

James Martin
Serrano-wrapped rabbit with chicory and orange salad

Wrapping the rabbit in Serrano ham adds flavour and retains moisture to ensure the meat doesn't dry out.

Ingredients Serves 4

Salad
6 heads of chicory, halved lengthways
4 oranges
1 tablespoon olive oil
1 teaspoon wholegrain mustard
1 tablespoon white wine vinegar
2 tablespoons extra virgin oil
1 bag of watercress

Rabbit
4 rabbit loins, fully trimmed
8 slices of Serrano ham
1 tablespoon olive oil

Method

Salad
Preheat the oven to 180°C/350°F/Gas 4 / Put the chicory into a roasting tin with the zest and juice of 1 orange and place in the oven for 5 minutes, until just tender / Remove the segments from the remaining oranges, reserving the juice, and place in a bowl / Heat a griddle pan and add the olive oil, then place the chicory, cut side down, on the griddle and cook for 1–2 minutes / Whisk together the mustard, 1 tablespoon of orange juice, the white wine vinegar and the extra virgin olive oil and season with salt and black pepper.

Rabbit
Season the rabbit with salt and black pepper / Wrap 2 pieces of Serrano ham around each rabbit loin / Heat a frying pan, add the olive oil and the rabbit and cook for 1–2 minutes on each side until golden, then remove from the heat and rest for 5 minutes in the pan.

To serve

Place the rabbit on a board and return the pan to the heat / Deglaze the pan with the remaining orange juice and then whisk the juices into the dressing / Place the chargrilled chicory on serving plates and scatter over the watercress and orange segments / Carve the rabbit into thick slices and place on top of the salad, then drizzle with a little dressing and serve.

Wine expert Peter Richards's choice
Gran Feudo Reserva Navarra

Theo Randall
Spatchcock pigeon roasted on bruschetta with cavolo nero, pancetta and porcini mushrooms

This might sound like a lot of meat, but squab is a small bird, just the right size for one person. You can also use wood pigeon for this recipe but it has a different flavour.

Ingredients Serves 4

Pigeon
4 squab pigeons, cleaned
110ml (4fl oz) Marsala
1 garlic clove, sliced
1 sprig of fresh thyme
2 tablespoons olive oil
4 slices of sourdough bread
6 slices of pancetta

Cavolo nero and porcini
2 heads of cavolo nero,
  leaves picked
4 tablespoons olive oil
2 garlic cloves, sliced
300g (11oz) fresh porcini
  mushrooms, cleaned

To serve

Juice of ½ lemon

Method

Pigeon
Place each pigeon on a board, cut down the backbone and force both sides away from each other / Turn over and push down on to the breasts with the palm of your hand to flatten the bird (the flatter it is, the more evenly it will cook) / Take the pigeons off the bone but leave the bones in the legs and the breasts joined together so you have four flat 2-breast, 2-leg pieces / Place in a bowl with all but 4 tablespoons of the Marsala, 1 garlic clove and the thyme, and leave to marinate for 1 hour / When ready to cook the pigeons, preheat the oven to 180°C/350°F/Gas 4 / Heat a heavy-based ovenproof frying pan, add the olive oil and the pigeons, skin side down / Cook for 1 minute on each side, then add the sourdough bread and slices of pancetta to the pan / Transfer everything to a baking tray and place in the oven for 6 minutes / Remove from the oven, place each pigeon on top of a slice of bread, skin side up, and return to the oven for a further 3 minutes.

Cavolo nero and porcini
Meanwhile, bring a pan of salted water to the boil, add the cavolo nero and cook for 1 minute, then drain and roughly chop / Heat a frying pan, add 2 tablespoons of olive oil, 1 garlic clove and the cavolo nero, and sauté for 5 minutes until tender / Heat the remainder of the olive oil and garlic in a frying pan, then add the porcini and cook for 3–4 minutes.

To serve

Place a slice of sourdough on each serving plate, top with some porcini and pile the cavolo nero alongside / Slice the pigeons in half lengthways and place on top, finishing with the pancetta / Add some of the remaining Marsala to the baking tray the pigeons were cooked in, and cook for 1 minute / Pour over the pigeons and serve, finishing with a little more lemon juice.

Wine expert Olly Smith's choice
Barbera d'Asti de Forville
This has a truffly note to it from the oak, which is going to pick up on the porcini. There's a bright tang on the finish and the acidity will marry with the lemon juice and the sourdough.

Si King
Spiced roasted guinea fowl served with a coconut and cucumber salad

This refreshing salad works a treat with the spicy flavours of the guinea fowl.

Ingredients Serves 4

Guinea fowl

4 guinea fowl breasts, boneless and skinless
1 teaspoon fennel seeds
1 teaspoon coriander seeds
4 cardamom pods, cracked and deseeded
2 tablespoons set yoghurt
1cm (½ inch) fresh root ginger, finely chopped
1 green chilli, deseeded and chopped
¼ teaspoon salt
½ teaspoon mace
A pinch of white pepper
1 tablespoon roughly chopped fresh coriander
1 tablespoon olive oil

Salad

1 cucumber, peeled, deseeded and sliced into ribbons with a vegetable peeler
2 tomatoes, cored, deseeded and diced
2 carrots, grated
1 red chilli, deseeded and finely chopped
200g (7oz) fresh coconut, grated
½ teaspoon palm sugar
Juice of ½ lemon
1 tablespoon olive oil
4 tablespoons fresh coriander leaves

Method

Guinea fowl

Preheat the oven to 180°C/350°F/Gas 4 / Slash the skin of the guinea fowl in 3 or 4 places to allow the spices to sink in / Place the fennel and coriander seeds in a frying pan and heat for 1 minute until just toasted / Put the seeds into a pestle and mortar with the cardamom seeds and crush to a powder / Put the yoghurt, ginger, chilli, salt, mace, pepper and fresh coriander into a bowl with the crushed seeds and mix thoroughly / Heat a frying pan, add the olive oil and the guinea fowl and cook for 1 minute on each side until golden / Transfer the guinea fowl to a roasting tray and divide the spice paste between the breasts, spreading it on the slashed sides / Place in the oven for 10–12 minutes, until cooked through.

Salad

While the guinea fowl is cooking, place the cucumber, tomatoes, carrots, chilli and coconut in a bowl and toss together / Whisk together the palm sugar, lemon juice and olive oil and drizzle over the salad.

To serve

Arrange the salad on four serving plates and top each with a cooked guinea fowl breast.

Wine expert Susie Barrie's choice

Tasmania Pinot Noir

This dish would work equally well with a white or red wine, as we need a medium-bodied, fruity wine that's not too heavy or too powerful. New World Pinots are basically just all about juicy fruit, and that's exactly what we have here.

Jun Tanaka

Smoked pigeon salad with beetroot, apples and walnuts

You'll be able to get smoking chips in the barbecue section of your local garden centre or DIY store. Experiment with different chips for different flavours.

Ingredients Serves 2

Pigeon
2 pigeons
2 tablespoons olive oil
25g (1oz) butter

Beetroot purée
25g (1oz) butter
250g (9oz) cooked beetroot, chopped
110ml (4fl oz) red port
50ml (2fl oz) red wine vinegar

Salad
250g (9oz) cooked beetroot, cut into 1cm (½ inch) cubes
1 Granny Smith apple, cut into 1cm (½ inch) cubes
25g (1oz) roasted walnuts, halved
½ red onion, finely chopped
1 tablespoon runny honey
50ml (2fl oz) walnut oil
50ml (2fl oz) Cabernet Sauvignon vinegar
50g (2oz) baby red chard

Method

Pigeon
Take the legs and breasts off the pigeons, and take the thigh bone out of the legs / Season the pigeon legs with salt and black pepper / Heat a small frying pan, add the olive oil and the boned legs, and cook on each side for 1–2 minutes / Put some smoking chips in the bottom of a steamer and place on the heat / When the chips are smoking add the pigeon breasts and smoke for 4 minutes / Heat a frying pan and add some olive oil / Take the pigeon breasts out of the smoker, season with salt and black pepper and place in the hot pan / Cook for 1 minute, add the butter, then turn over and cook for a further minute.

Beetroot purée
While the pigeon breasts are smoking, heat a saucepan, add the butter, beetroot, port and vinegar and cook for 3–4 minutes / Season with salt and black pepper, then place in a blender and blitz to a purée / Pass the purée through a sieve and keep warm.

Salad
Mix together all the ingredients except the red chard in a bowl and season with salt and black pepper.

To serve

Spoon the beetroot purée on to the plate and arrange the pieces of pigeon on top / Spoon the salad alongside the pigeon and top with the red chard.

Wine expert Olly Smith's choice
Scotchman's Hill Swan Bay Pinot Noir
Pinot Noir typically has aromas and flavours of red and black berries when it's young, and more earthy, savoury qualities when it's older. This one has still got its youthful verve.

Nick Nairn
Warm mallard salad with puy lentils and crispy parsnips

If you are using wild duck for this, make sure you go to a reputable supplier. Ask your butcher where they source their game.

Ingredients Serves 4

Sauce
1 mallard duck carcass, roughly chopped
25g (1oz) butter
2 shallots, sliced
2 garlic cloves, crushed
1 bay leaf
1 sprig of fresh thyme
1 tablespoon tomato purée
150 ml (5fl oz) red wine
800 ml (14fl oz) chicken stock

Lentils
50g (2oz) Puy lentils
1 garlic clove, crushed
1 sprig of fresh thyme
150ml (5fl oz) chicken stock

Duck
1 tablespoon sunflower oil
4 mallard duck breasts

Parsnips
150–175g (5–6oz) parsnips, thinly sliced lengthways with a vegetable peeler

To serve
150–175g (5–6oz) mixed salad leaves
1 tablespoon balsamic vinegar
2 tablespoons extra virgin olive oil

Method

Sauce
Preheat the oven to 230°C/450°F/Gas 8 / Put the mallard carcass into a roasting tin and roast for 15 minutes, until browned / Heat a frying pan, add half the butter, and when foaming brown, add the shallots, garlic, bay leaf and thyme / Season with salt and black pepper and cook until everything is well browned / Add the tomato purée and cook until dry / Pour in the wine to deglaze the pan, and cook until all the liquid has gone / Add the roasted carcass and stir to coat, then add the stock and 200ml (7fl oz) of water / Bring to the boil, then reduce the heat and simmer very gently until thickened (approximately 45 minutes) / Pass the sauce through a fine sieve and skim off any fat, then set aside and keep warm.

Lentils
While the sauce is simmering, put the lentils, garlic, thyme and stock into a saucepan over a very low heat / Add just enough water to cover, and cook very gently for 20 minutes, until the lentils are tender / Drain the lentils, put them into a bowl and keep them warm until required.

Duck
When the sauce and lentils are ready, season the duck breasts well with salt and black pepper / Heat a large frying pan, add a splash of sunflower oil and add the breasts, skin side down / Cook for 4–5 minutes, until crisp and brown, then cook on the other side for 2–4 minutes, leaving the centre pink / Remove to a plate and allow the duck to rest in a warm place for at least 10 minutes.

Parsnips
While the duck breasts are resting, heat a deep-fat fryer to 190°C / Deep fry the parsnip slices until golden, then drain, sprinkle with salt and leave them on kitchen paper until required.

To serve
Toss the salad leaves in a large bowl with the vinegar, oil and lentils / Carve the duck breast into thin slices and add them to the salad / Carefully toss with your hands and divide between serving plates, then carefully drizzle over some of the sauce / Top each plate with a handful of fried parsnip slices and serve immediately.

Wine expert Susie Barrie's choice
Muriel Rioja Crianza
This is a warming, comforting wine with plummy, creamy flavours that will go brilliantly with the duck, the dressing and the crispy skin.

Matt Tebbutt
Spiced marinated rabbit with herbed couscous and pine nuts

Rabbit is cheap and healthy, so don't be put off, give it a try. This is a great, simple recipe that's guaranteed to convert any doubters.

Ingredients Serves 4

Rabbit
1 tablespoon cumin seeds
1 tablespoon coriander seeds
½ tablespoon black
   peppercorns
½ tablespoon white
   peppercorns
1 dried chilli
5 tablespoons extra virgin
   olive oil
3 garlic cloves, crushed
2 tablespoons finely chopped
   fresh coriander roots
2 tablespoons finely chopped
   fresh mint leaves
2 rabbit loins

Couscous
110g (4oz) couscous
110ml (4fl oz) Cabernet
   Sauvignon vinegar
3–4 banana shallots, thinly
   sliced into rounds
2 tablespoons caster sugar
4 piquillo peppers, finely
   diced
3 tablespoons pine nuts,
   toasted
1 bunch of fresh coriander,
   roughly chopped
1 bunch of fresh mint, roughly
   chopped

Method

Rabbit
Heat a frying pan, add the cumin and coriander seeds, peppercorns and chilli, and toast for 1–2 minutes / Put them into a pestle and mortar and crush, then transfer them to a large bowl / Add the olive oil, garlic, coriander and mint and mix well / Add the rabbit loins to the bowl, massage the spicy marinade well into the meat, then set aside at room temperature for a few hours / When ready to cook the rabbit, wipe off a little of the marinade, leaving the meat just coated / Heat a frying pan, add the rabbit and cook on each side for 2–3 minutes.

Couscous
Just before you start to cook the rabbit, place the couscous in a bowl and pour boiling water over to just cover / Cover with clingfilm and set aside for 5 minutes / Meanwhile, place the vinegar and sugar in a small saucepan, bring to a simmer and cook for 1 minute, until the sugar has dissolved / Remove from the heat, add the shallots, toss to coat, then set aside / Remove the clingfilm from the couscous and run a fork through the grains / Add the peppers, pine nuts, coriander and mint and mix well / Add the shallots and the vinegar mixture and season with salt and black pepper.

To serve

Place a spoonful of couscous in the centre of each serving plate / Slice the rabbit and arrange on top of the couscous / Spoon over any meat juices there may be in the pan.

Wine expert Susy Atkins's choice
Tyrrell's Old Winery Pinot Noir
Those spices call for a warming winter red. This is delicious, really rounded, really easy-going but packed with red berry fruit, which will work so well with that hint of chilli.

Vivek Singh
Peanut and dried mango crusted partridge with a curry leaf and tomato quinoa

Northern India has a great tradition of game cooking, and Vivek is renowned for his game dishes.

Ingredients Serves 4

Partridge
1 teaspoon salt
2 tablespoons malt vinegar
2 tablespoons ginger and garlic paste, or equal quantities of ginger and garlic pastes mixed with a little water
4 partridges, halved lengthways
1 teaspoon cumin seeds
200ml (7fl oz) Greek yoghurt
2 teaspoons dried mango powder
3 tablespoons roasted unsalted peanuts, coarsely crushed
2 fresh hot green chillies, deseeded and finely chopped
1 tablespoon vegetable oil
2 tablespoons finely chopped coriander stems
Juice of ½ lemon

Quinoa
150g (5oz) quinoa
3 tablespoons vegetable or corn oil
1 dried red chilli, broken into 3 pieces
1 teaspoon mustard seeds
20 fresh curry leaves
1 large onion, finely chopped
1 green chilli, deseeded and finely chopped
1cm (½ inch) piece of fresh root ginger, finely chopped
2 tomatoes, roughly chopped
1½ teaspoons salt
1 teaspoon red chilli powder
½ teaspoon sugar
1 tablespoon finely chopped fresh coriander or basil
Juice of ½ lemon

Method

Partridge
Preheat the oven to 200°C/400°F/Gas 6 and preheat the grill to high / Whisk together the salt, malt vinegar and ginger and garlic paste in a small bowl / Spoon over the partridges and leave to marinate for a few minutes / Meanwhile, heat a frying pan, add the cumin seeds and dry-fry until just toasted / Lightly crush them, using a pestle and mortar, then place them in a bowl with the yoghurt, dried mango powder, crushed roasted peanuts, chopped green chillies and oil, and whisk together / Add the coriander and spread the mixture over the partridges – if you have time, leave to marinate for 30 minutes / Thread the partridges on to soaked wooden skewers, place on a baking tray and put into the oven for 3-4 minutes / Remove them from the oven and place them under the hot grill for 3 minutes / Remove the partridges from the skewers and set aside to rest.

Quinoa
While the partridges are marinating in the yoghurt, soak the quinoa in cold water for 15 minutes, then drain and rinse / Place in a saucepan with 300ml of salted water, then bring to the boil and simmer for about 15 minutes, until the grains are cooked but still retain some bite – quinoa develops a white ring round the circumference of each grain when it is about ready / Drain off any excess water / Heat the oil in a heavy-based pan and add the red chilli and mustard seeds / Let them crackle and splutter for about 30 seconds, then add the curry leaves / As soon as the leaves are crisp, add the onion and cook for 3-4 minutes, until starting to turn golden / Now add the green chilli and ginger and stir for 1 minute / Add the tomatoes, salt and chilli powder and cook over a medium heat for 3-4 minutes, until most of the moisture from the tomato has evaporated and the mixture begins to come together / Add the cooked quinoa and mix for 1-2 minutes, until heated through / Finish by stirring in the sugar, coriander or basil and the lemon juice.

To serve

Spoon the quinoa into the centre of your serving plates and top each one with 2 partridge halves.

Wine expert Olly Smith's choice
The Ned Pinot Grigio
This is no ordinary Pinot Grigio – it's got a little pinky hue like an onion skin that tells you it's going to have a greater intensity of both aroma and flavour. Peachy, with real fruitiness. Phenomenal.

Antonio Carluccio
Fillet of venison and wild mushroom sauce

This dish, from the Italian region of Umbria, needs a bit of forward planning but it's worth it. The summer truffles used here have a more delicate flavour than winter truffles.

Ingredients Serves 4

Venison

500g (18oz) fillet of venison, trimmed and cut into 2.5cm (1 inch) thick medallions
5 tablespoons extra virgin olive oil
1 tablespoon balsamic vinegar (non-aged)
1 carrot, finely diced
1 onion, finely diced

Sauce

110g (4oz) butter
2 small onions, very finely sliced
40g (1½oz) dried morels, soaked in warm water for 2 hours (reserve the water)
150g (5oz) fresh porcini mushrooms, thickly sliced
2 tablespoons balsamic vinegar (aged for 10–15 years)
4 tablespoons dry sherry
6 tablespoons double cream

To serve

1 summer truffle

Method

Venison

The day before cooking, place the venison in a dish and cover with 3 tablespoons of the olive oil, the balsamic vinegar, carrot and onion / Season with salt and pepper and place in the fridge overnight / When ready to cook, remove the venison from the marinade, pat dry and season with salt and black pepper / Heat a frying pan, add the remaining olive oil and the venison and fry on each side for 3 minutes, until brown on the outside, pink on the inside.

Sauce

About 20 minutes before you start to cook the venison, heat a frying pan, add the butter and onions and fry the onion until translucent / Add the pre-soaked morels and cook for 10 minutes / Add the porcini and fry for a further 3–5 minutes / Add the balsamic vinegar, sherry, cream and some salt and black pepper, and cook gently for 10 minutes / The sauce may become quite thick, so add a little of the morel soaking water to the pan.

To serve

Spoon the sauce and mushrooms on to serving plates, and top with the venison / Shave the truffle over the top.

Wine expert Susie Barrie's choice
Baron de Ley Rioja Reserva
As long as you choose a wine that isn't too light and delicate, you can basically go for whatever grape variety and country you personally like for this dish. This wine is plummy, creamy, smooth and spicy.

James Martin
Breaded pheasant breast with beetroot purée and marinated beetroot

Beetroot isn't used enough. Take care when peeling it or you may be left with stained hands!

Ingredients Serves 4

Marinated beetroot

350g (12oz) cooked beetroot, cut into wedges
30g (1¼ oz) shallots, finely chopped
2 tablespoons finely chopped fresh flat-leaf parsley
2 tablespoons finely chopped fresh chervil
2 tablespoons finely chopped fresh chives
3 tablespoons aged balsamic vinegar
4 tablespoons extra virgin olive oil

Beetroot purée

600g (1lb 5oz) raw beetroot, peeled and cut into chunks
1 onion, roughly chopped
½ garlic clove, roughly chopped
2 sprigs of fresh thyme, leaves picked

Pheasant

4 pheasant breasts, boneless and skinless
75g (3oz) plain flour
1 egg, beaten
50g (2oz) breadcrumbs
25g (1oz) butter
1 teaspoon olive oil

Method

Marinated beetroot

Toss all the ingredients together in a bowl and season with salt and black pepper / Place in the fridge and leave for at least 1 hour, preferably longer.

Beetroot purée

While the beetroot is marinating, place everything for the purée into a food processor and blend until smooth / Place a frying pan on the heat and add the purée / Cook over a low heat for 30–40 minutes, stirring occasionally, until the beetroot is tender / Season with salt and black pepper.

Pheasant

When the beetroot purée is nearly ready, place the pheasant breasts on a board, cover with clingfilm and tap gently to flatten out / Season with salt and black pepper / Place the flour, egg and breadcrumbs in separate shallow bowls, and dip the pheasant breasts first into the flour, then into the egg and finally into the breadcrumbs, coating thoroughly in each / Heat a frying pan, add the butter and oil, then add the pheasant and fry on each side until golden, 1–2 minutes on each side.

To serve

Place a spoonful of beetroot purée in the centre of each serving plate / Cut the pheasant breasts in half lengthways and place on top of the purée / Spoon the marinated beetroot alongside.

Wine expert Tim Atkin's choice
Muga Rosado Rioja

Marcus Wareing
Roasted quail with watermelon, spring onion fondue, cobnuts and quail vinaigrette

Cobnuts are only available in Autumn; if you can't get hold of them you can use hazelnuts instead.

Ingredients Serves 2

Quail vinaigrette
1 tablespoon olive oil
2 large shallots, finely sliced
2 quail legs
2 sprigs of fresh thyme
2 sprigs of fresh rosemary
500ml (18fl oz) brown chicken stock
75ml (3fl oz) extra virgin olive oil
75ml (3fl oz) white wine vinegar

Roasted quail
500ml (18fl oz) chicken stock
4 sprigs of fresh thyme
½ head of garlic
3 quails, legs removed
1 tablespoon light olive oil
25g (1oz) butter, diced

Spring onion fondue
25g (1oz) butter
1 garlic clove
1 bay leaf
8 spring onions, cut into fine julienne strips
1 tablespoon chicken stock

To serve
1 slice watermelon, diced into 0.5cm (¼ inch) cubes
Olive oil
25g (1oz) cobnuts, finely sliced

Method

Quail vinaigrette
Heat the olive oil in a medium pan over a moderate heat, add the shallots and cook for 1 minute / Add the quail legs and fry until golden / Add the thyme and rosemary and enough chicken stock to cover / Bring to the boil, then reduce the heat and simmer for 20 minutes / Strain the stock through a sieve and return to the pan / Bring back to the boil and reduce down to a thick consistency until there is about 75ml (3fl oz) left / Whisk in the olive oil and vinegar and season with salt and black pepper.

Quail
While the quail legs are cooking, place the chicken stock, thyme and garlic in a saucepan and bring to a simmer / Add the quail and simmer for 2½ minutes, then remove from the pan and drain on kitchen paper / Heat a frying pan and add the oil and butter / Add the quail, skin side down, and fry for 3–5 minutes, until there is moderate resistance when the bottom of the breast is squeezed / Remove from the pan and set aside to rest for 5 minutes.

Spring onion fondue
When the quail is nearly ready, put the butter, garlic and bay leaf into a medium saucepan over a moderate heat / When the butter has melted, add the spring onions and cook for 3 minutes / Add the stock and cook for a further 5 minutes until the spring onions are al dente – they should not colour at all / Remove the garlic and bay leaf and keep the fondue warm.

To serve
Toss the watermelon with a little olive oil and some black pepper / Place 3 spoonfuls of the fondue on to each serving plate and top with a warm quail breast / Sprinkle a little sliced cobnut on each quail breast / Scatter the watermelon around the plate and spoon over the quail vinaigrette.

Wine expert Peter Richards's choice
Château Complazens, Syrah
With this wine what you get is loads of gorgeous meaty, peppery, gamey aromas, which will match really well with the bird. It's the kind of wine that really needs food to work.

Tom Kitchin
Roast teal, purple sprouting broccoli and salsify

Teal is a small, wild duck found in Britain all year round. It's worth trying to source it, as you'll taste the difference to farmed duck.

Ingredients Serves 4

Teal
75g (3oz) butter
1 tablespoon olive oil
8 teal, cleaned and wishbone removed
200ml (7fl oz) game jus

Broccoli and salsify
6 salsify, washed and dried
Juice of 1 lemon
250ml (9fl oz) chicken stock
450g (1lb) purple sprouting broccoli
200g (7oz) pancetta, cut into lardons
75g (3oz) plain flour

Method

Teal
Preheat the oven to 220°C/425°F/Gas 7 / Heat a frying pan, add a little of the butter and the olive oil and seal the teal on each side / Transfer the birds to a roasting tray and place in the oven and roast for 8–10 minutes, then remove them from the tray and set aside to rest for a few minutes / Heat the teal roasting tray on the hob, add the game jus and deglaze the pan.

Broccoli and salsify
While the teal is resting heat a deep fat fryer to 180°C / Peel 4 of the salsify into lemon water to prevent oxidisation, then slice thickly / Heat a frying pan, add the remaining butter, lemon juice and salsify and sauté for a couple of minutes / Add the chicken stock, bring to a simmer and cook until tender – about 3–4 minutes / Bring a pan of salted water to the boil, add the broccoli and cook for 2 minutes / Drain and refresh in cold water, then drain once more / Heat a frying pan, add the pancetta, cook for 1 minute, then add the cooked salsify and broccoli and toss together to heat through / Cut the remaining salsify (leaving the skin on) into ribbons and gently dust them with the flour / Drop them into the deep-fat fryer and fry until golden.

To serve

Carve the breasts from the birds / Pile the salsify and broccoli into the centre of your serving plates and place the teal breasts on top / Top with the fried salsify and a spoonful of game jus.

Wine expert Olly Smith's choice
The Red Mullet
This is a special blend of Tempranillo, Grenache, Shiraz and Mourvèdre grapes. It's got a great balance between red fruit and black fruit. It's not too heavy but it's by no means a wimp.

Lawrence Keogh
Roast pheasant with sherry glazed parsnips and chestnuts

These parsnips are particularly good and will go with almost anything, they're even delicious on their own!

Ingredients Serves 2

Pheasant
1 pheasant (hen if possible, as they are fattier)
50g (2oz) butter

Parsnips and chestnuts
800g (1lb 12oz) parsnips, peeled and cut into 7cm (3 inch) batons
250ml (9fl oz) dry sherry
75g (3oz) soft brown sugar
110g (4oz) butter
10 chestnuts, roasted, peeled and roughly chopped
1 small bunch of fresh flat-leaf parsley, chopped

To serve
1 small bunch of watercress

Method

Pheasant
Preheat the oven to 220°C/425°F/Gas 7 / Remove the legs and wishbone of the pheasant / Season thoroughly inside and out with salt and black pepper / Heat a frying pan, add the butter and the pheasant and seal on each side until golden / Place in the oven for about 10 minutes, then remove and set aside to rest.

Parsnips and chestnuts
At the same time, place the parsnips, sherry, sugar and butter in an earthenware dish or roasting tin and toss together / Place in the oven for 15–20 minutes, until golden and tender / Remove from the oven, place on the hob, bring to a simmer, then reduce the liquid down to a thick glaze / Add the chestnuts and parsley and toss together / Season with salt and black pepper.

To serve
Carve the breast from the pheasant / Spoon the parsnips into the centre of your serving plates / Top with the pheasant and add a handful of watercress.

Wine expert Peter Richards's choice
Les Vieilles Vignes de Chateau Maris
This is a special occasion kind of wine. There's loads of rich, ripe fruit there, but essentially it's a savoury style of wine that will go really well with the richness of the meat and the saltiness of the sherry.

Si King
Loin of venison with a blackberry and sloe gin glaze served with clapshot rösti and parsnip crisps

Clapshot is a Scottish potato cake, and this is Si's tasty interpretation of a classic dish.

Ingredients Serves 4

Venison
250g (9oz) smoked streaky bacon
1 kg (2lb 2oz) venison loin, trimmed
1 tablespoon olive oil
110ml (4fl oz) chicken stock
110g (4oz) blackberries
1 tablespoon sloe gin

Rösti
500g (1lb 2oz) old potatoes, grated
500g (1lb 2oz) turnip, grated
250g (9oz) carrot, grated
50g (2oz) butter, melted
2 teaspoons olive oil

Parsnip crisps
Vegetable oil
1 parsnip, thinly sliced

Beans and peas
200g (7oz) green beans
150g (5oz) sugar snap peas
Olive oil

Method

Venison
Stretch the bacon using the back of a knife until really thin / Cut the loin into pieces about 2cm (¾ inch) thick / Wrap a piece of bacon around the side of each medallion of venison, securing it with a toothpick / Heat a frying pan, add the oil then fry the venison on each side for about 3 minutes / Remove from the pan and set aside to rest on a plate / Add the stock to the pan and deglaze, rubbing the bottom of the pan to incorporate the caramelised meat juices / Add the blackberries and poach for 2 minutes, mashing lightly with the back of a fork / Add the sloe gin and bring to the boil, then simmer for a further 2 minutes / Season with salt and black pepper.

Rösti
While the venison is cooking, mix the vegetables together and place in a clean tea towel / Roll the tea towel tightly into a ball and squeeze out all the liquid / Break up the compressed ball of vegetables, place in a bowl and add the melted butter / Season with salt and black pepper and mix well / Form the rösti into a cake about 1cm (½ inch) thick / Heat a frying pan and add the olive oil and the rösti / Cook for 2–3 minutes on each side, until golden and crispy but tender in the middle.

Parsnip crisps
When the venison and rösti are nearly ready, heat a deep-sided frying pan and add sufficient vegetable oil to cover the base 3cm (1¼ inches) deep / Drop the parsnip slices into the hot oil and fry until golden, then drain on kitchen paper.

Beans and peas
At the same time bring a pan of water to the boil, and cook the beans for 3–4 minutes and the sugar snap peas for 2 minutes / Drain and toss with a little olive oil, salt and black pepper.

To serve

Place a wedge of rösti in the centre of each serving plate / Top with the venison, a spoonful of sauce and some parsnip crisps and arrange the greens alongside.

Wine expert Olly Smith's choice
De Martino Legado Reserva Syrah
This is all about black fruit, and those brambly and sloe flavours that are exactly what are in Si's dish, so it's going to work perfectly. The meaty quality of this wine is just the ticket.

Ingredients Serves 4

Venison

1 tablespoon English mustard
1 tablespoon honey
1 tablespoon vegetable oil
600g (1Ib 5oz) venison fillet, trimmed, rolled in clingfilm and cut into 4 pieces
1 tablespoon finely chopped fresh root ginger
1 tablespoon black sesame seeds
1 tablespoon white sesame seeds
1 tablespoon coriander seeds, coarsely ground

Pear chutney

2 pears, peeled, cored and chopped
1 Granny Smith apple, peeled, cored and chopped
½ teaspoon grated fresh root ginger
½ red onion, thinly sliced
1 bay leaf
1 star anise
2.5cm (1 inch) piece of cinnamon stick
5 cloves
10 black peppercorns
75g (3oz) dark brown sugar
75ml (3fl oz) cider vinegar
50ml (2fl oz) water

Parsnip chips

4 small parsnips, peeled and cut lengthways into 4
2 tablespoons honey
2 sprigs of fresh lemon thyme
Crushed black peppercorns

To serve

3–4 tablespoons meat jus or well aged balsamic vinegar

Atul Kochhar
Spiced venison with pear chutney and sweet spicy parsnip

We should all try to incorporate more game into our diets. It's healthier and leaner than most other meats and we can be sure it's led a happier life.

Method

Venison

Preheat the oven to 180°C/350°F/Gas 4 / Mix together all the venison ingredients, apart from the oil, to make a paste / Heat a frying pan, add the oil and sear the meat at either end / Cut away the clingfilm, then brush the meat liberally with the paste / Place in the oven for 12–15 minutes, depending on how you like your meat / Remove from the oven and rest the meat on a rack.

Pear chutney

While the venison is in the oven, heat a frying pan, add all the ingredients and mix well / Cook for 5–8 minutes, until the pears are soft / Remove from the heat, cool slightly then store the chutney in a sterilized airtight jar until required.

Parsnip chips

While the venison is resting, heat a deep-fat fryer to 190°C / Put the parsnip chips into the fryer and cook for 3–4 minutes, until golden and tender, then drain on kitchen paper / Meanwhile, put the honey into a small saucepan and gently heat with the remaining ingredients / When hot, toss the parsnips in the honey.

To serve

Cut the venison into slices and arrange on serving plates / Place a pile of parsnip chips on the side, with a spoonful of chutney / Finish with a drizzle of meat jus or balsamic vinegar.

Wine expert Susie Barrie's choice
Château St Martin de la Garrigue Bronzinelle
This wine is a blend of grape varieties, and it has a really herbal, savoury character that is just perfect with meat. It's got some lovely plummy fruit overtones to match the pear chutney.

James Martin
Roasted partridge with creamed Brussels sprouts and chestnuts

This is for all you Brussels sprout haters – try these and you'll be converted.

Ingredients Serves 4

Partridge
4 partridges, cleaned and halved lengthways
1 tablespoon olive oil
25g (1oz) butter

Sprouts
50g butter
1 tablespoon olive oil
2 shallots, finely sliced
300g (11oz) Brussels sprouts, trimmed and finely sliced
2 sprigs of fresh thyme
110ml (4fl oz) white wine
200ml (7fl oz) double cream
150g (5oz) cooked chestnuts, roughly chopped
3 tablespoons chopped fresh flat-leaf parsley

Sauce
75g (3oz) butter
1 shallot, finely chopped
75ml (3fl oz) red wine
175ml (6fl oz) chicken stock

Method

Partridge
Preheat the oven to 220°C/425°F/Gas 7 / Season the partridges with salt and black pepper / Heat a frying pan, add the olive oil and butter and add the partridges skin side down / Cook for 1–2 minutes on each side until golden, then transfer to a roasting tin and place in the oven for 12–15 minutes / Remove from the oven and set aside to rest.

Sprouts
While the partridges are resting, heat the butter and oil in a frying pan / Add the shallots and fry for 1–2 minutes, then add the sprouts and stir-fry for 1 minute / Add the thyme and white wine and bring to a simmer / Cook for 2 minutes, then add the cream and cook for a further 2 minutes / Add the chestnuts, season with salt and black pepper, and stir in the parsley.

Sauce
Meanwhile, heat a second frying pan, add half the butter and the shallot and sauté for 2 minutes / Add the wine and bring to the boil, then reduce the heat and cook until reduced by half / Add the chicken stock and bring back to the boil / Simmer for 3 minutes, until the sauce has reduced and thickened slightly / Season with salt and black pepper, then whisk in the rest of the butter.

To serve
Pile the sprouts in the centre of your serving plates, and top each one with 2 halves of partridge / Spoon the red wine sauce round the edge.

Wine expert Peter Richards's choice
Olarra Clasico Rioja Crianza

James Martin
Wild boar pie with roast parsnips

Wild boar is becoming increasingly available and the difference in taste to pork is worth the extra pennies.

Ingredients Serves 4–6

Pie

1kg (2lb 2oz) wild boar shoulder, trimmed and cut into large cubes
2 tablespoons olive oil
175g (6oz) smoked pancetta, cut into lardons
225g (8oz) small shallots, peeled and left whole
400g (14oz) carrots, cut into large chunks
175g (6oz) chestnut mushrooms
2 bay leaves
2 sprigs of fresh flat-leaf parsley
2 tablespoons plain flour
200ml (7fl oz) red wine
650ml (18fl oz) beef stock
500g (1lb 2oz) all-butter puff pastry
1 egg, beaten

Parsnips

4–5 large parsnips, peeled and cut into chunks
3 tablespoons olive oil

Method

Pie

Season the wild boar with salt and black pepper / Heat a large casserole dish, then add the olive oil and wild boar in batches and fry until well browned on all sides / Set the meat aside and add the pancetta to the pan / Fry for 1–2 minutes until it releases some fat, then add the shallots, carrots and mushrooms and fry for 2 minutes / Add the bay leaves and parsley and return the meat to the pan / Add the flour and mix well to coat everything / Add the wine, deglaze the pan, then bring to the boil and reduce by a quarter / Add the beef stock and return it to a gentle simmer / Cover with a lid, check to make sure it is just simmering gently, then cook for 2 hours until the meat is very tender / Check the seasoning, spoon into a pie dish and leave to cool for at least 30 minutes / When ready to cook the pie, preheat the oven to 190°C/375°F/Gas 5 / Roll the pastry to 5mm (¼ inch) thick / Brush the rim and outside edge of the dish with beaten egg, then lay the pastry over the top / Press the sides down and trim about 2cm (¾ inch) down around the edge, so the pastry sticks to the outside of the pie dish / Use any trimmings to decorate the top of the pie / Brush with beaten egg and make 2 slits with a knife in the centre / Place in the oven for 30–45 minutes, until golden brown and piping hot.

Parsnips

When the pie has been in the oven for about 15 minutes, season the parsnips with salt and black pepper, place on a baking tray and toss with the olive oil / Place in the oven with the pie and roast for 20–25 minutes, turning occasionally, until golden and tender.

To serve

Spoon the pie on to serving plates and pile the parsnips alongside.

Wine expert Olly Smith's choice
Porcupine Ridge Syrah

James Martin
Roasted duck with plum sauce and steamed Asian greens

James Martin
Breaded chicken escalope with sauce Grebiche, sautéd courgettes and cherry tomatoes

James Martin
Caponata with turkey escalope

Dave Myers
Mediterranean chicken roulade with mushroom orzo and rocket salad

Rachel Allen
Chicken and pilaf with green salad

Silvena Rowe
Pomegranate glazed duck with bulgar, chickpea and pomegranate pilaf

James Martin
Spiced tadeek rice with Moroccan rice-coated chicken and preserved lemon salad

Ken Hom
Garlic chicken with cucumber and spicy Sichuan noodles

Paul Rankin
Spiced chicken livers with Chinese noodles, soy, black pepper and cream

Nic Watt
Grilled poussin marinated in ume shu and miso with a pickle salad

Daniel Galmiche
Pan-roasted chicken breast with leeks and potatoes

Raymond Blanc
Poached chicken with a fricassée of wild mushrooms

Patrick Williams
Jerk Kiev with yam forestière

Theo Randall
Boned chicken stuffed with prosciutto, mascarpone and rosemary, served with purple sprouting and romanesco broccoli

James Martin
Chorizo chicken with sautéd chorizo, potatoes and spinach

Si King
Festive duck breast with pancetta, Savoy cabbage and mash

Jun Tanaka
Salt crust chicken with peas, broad beans and mousseron mushrooms

Daniel Galmiche
Lemon chicken casserole

Poultry

James Martin
Roasted duck with plum sauce and steamed Asian greens

A tasty twist on a Chinese favourite –
the plum sauce works well with pork too.

Ingredients Serves 4–6

Duck
1 x 2kg (2lb 4oz) duck
2 tablespoons olive oil

Sauce
1 tablespoon olive oil
3 spring onions, sliced
3 star anise
1 cinnamon stick
½ teaspoon Sichuan
     peppercorns
500g (1lb 2oz) plums,
     quartered and stoned
125ml (5fl oz) rice wine
     vinegar
75g (3oz) caster sugar

Greens
500g (1lb 2oz) mixed Asian
     greens (bok choi, pak choi,
     young kale, etc.)
2 spring onions, sliced
     diagonally
2 small bunches of fresh
     coriander
3cm (1¼ inches) fresh root
     ginger, peeled and cut into
     julienne strips

Method

Duck
Preheat the oven to 220°C/425°F/Gas 7 / Place the duck on a rack over a deep roasting tin and pierce the skin all over with a knife / Pour a kettle of boiling water over the duck, then drain off the water and discard / Rub the duck with the olive oil and season with salt and black pepper / Place in the oven for 1½ hours, until crispy, golden and cooked through / Remove from the oven and rest for 10 minutes, uncovered.

Sauce
When the duck is nearly ready to come out of the oven, heat a deep-sided frying pan and add the olive oil and the spring onions / Fry for 1 minute until just softened, then add the spices / Stir-fry for a further minute, then add the plums and stir to combine / Add the vinegar and sugar and bring to the boil, then cover and simmer for 5 minutes, until the plums have softened / Remove from the heat and remove the star anise and cinnamon / Place the mixture in a blender or food-processor and blitz to a purée / Pass through a sieve into a bowl and season with a little salt and black pepper.

Greens
While the duck is resting, fill a wok two-thirds full of water, place a bamboo steamer on top, and bring the water to the boil / Place the greens in the steamer and sprinkle with the spring onions, coriander and ginger / Cover with a lid and steam for 3–4 minutes, until just tender.

To serve

Ladle a good spoonful of plum sauce into the centre of each serving plate and tap gently to settle it into a circle / Top with the steamed greens / Carve the duck and place on top of the greens.

Wine expert Peter Richards' choice
Concha y Toro Winemakers Lot Malbec

James Martin
Breaded chicken escalope with sauce Grebiche, sautéd courgettes and cherry tomatoes

Japanese breadcrumbs give a lovely, crisp coating, but don't worry if you can't find them – any breadcrumbs will do.

Ingredients Serves 4

Chicken
4 chicken breasts, boneless and skinless
75g (3oz) plain flour
2 eggs, beaten
60g (2½oz) Japanese breadcrumbs
2 tablespoons olive oil
50g (2oz) butter
4 tablespoons olive oil

Courgettes and tomatoes
2 tablespoons olive oil
50g (2oz) butter
2–3 large courgettes, diced
2 sprigs of fresh rosemary, finely chopped
175g (6oz) cherry tomatoes

Sauce
1 banana shallot, finely diced
1 garlic clove
75g (3oz) gherkins, finely diced
4 tablespoons capers, rinsed
3 tablespoons roughly chopped fresh flat-leaf parsley

Method

Chicken
Place each chicken breast on a board lined with clingfilm and cover with more clingfilm / Using a meat hammer or rolling pin, bash the chicken until it is just 5mm (¼ inch) thick / Remove the clingfilm and season the chicken with salt and black pepper / Season the flour with salt and black pepper / Put the flour, beaten egg and breadcrumbs into 3 separate shallow bowls / Dip the chicken first into the flour, then into the egg and finally into the breadcrumbs, making sure you coat each side thoroughly / Heat the oil and butter in a large frying pan / Add the chicken breasts, one at a time, and fry until golden – about 2 minutes on each side / Once all the chicken has been cooked, set it aside to keep warm but don't wash the pan.

Courgettes and tomatoes
Heat the oil and butter in a large frying pan and add the courgettes and rosemary / Sauté for 3–4 minutes, until just golden and beginning to soften / Add the tomatoes and cook for a further 2 minutes / Season with salt and black pepper.

Sauce
When the courgettes are cooked, reheat the pan you cooked the chicken in, add the shallots and garlic and fry for 1 minute / Add the gherkins and capers and cook for a further minute / Season with salt and black pepper and add the parsley.

To serve

Serve the chicken with the sauce spooned over and a pile of courgettes and tomatoes alongside.

James Martin
Caponata with turkey escalope

Caponata is a traditional Sicilian accompaniment but it's also delicious served on its own with toasted ciabatta.

Ingredients Serves 4

Caponata
8–10 tablespoons olive oil
750g (1lb 10oz) aubergines, roughly chopped
1 onion, finely sliced
3 celery sticks, thinly sliced
400g/14oz tinned chopped tomatoes
125g (4½oz) pitted large green olives
75g (3oz) capers, drained
2 tablespoons caster sugar
4 tablespoons red wine vinegar

Turkey
4 thin slices of turkey breast
75g (3oz) plain flour
2 eggs, beaten
150g (5oz) breadcrumbs
2–3 tablespoons vegetable oil

Method

Caponata
Heat a large frying pan, add the olive oil and the aubergines in batches and fry for 2–3 minutes, until softened and golden / Remove from the pan and set aside / Add the onions to the pan and fry for 2 minutes until just softened, then add the celery and fry for a further minute / Add the chopped tomatoes and bring to a simmer / Add the olives, capers and cooked aubergines to the pan and return to a simmer / Cook for 3–4 minutes, then add the sugar and vinegar and season with salt and black pepper / Remove from the pan and set aside to cool to room temperature.

Turkey
While the caponata is cooling, place each turkey slice on a board lined with clingfilm and cover with more clingfilm / Using a meat hammer or rolling pin, bash the turkey until each slice is just 5mm (¼ inch) thick / Remove the clingfilm and season the turkey with salt and black pepper / Place the flour, beaten egg and breadcrumbs in 3 separate shallow bowls / Dip the turkey first into the flour, then into the egg and finally into the breadcrumbs, making sure you coat each side thoroughly / Heat a frying pan and add the oil and the turkey escalopes, in batches if necessary / Fry for 2–3 minutes on each side over a medium heat, until golden brown and cooked through.

To serve

Place a turkey escalope on each serving plate and spoon some caponata alongside.

Wine expert Susy Atkins's choice
Fairleigh Estate Sauvignon Blanc

Dave Myers
Mediterranean chicken roulade with mushroom orzo and rocket salad

Orzo is a particular type of rice-shaped pasta. You might need to go to an Italian deli if you can't find it in your local supermarket.

Ingredients Serves 4

Chicken
4 chicken breasts, boneless and skinless
4 thin slices of pancetta
12 basil leaves
110g (4oz) dolcelatte, cut into 12 strips
4 baby plum tomatoes, halved
2 tablespoons olive oil

Orzo
10g (½oz) dried porcini mushrooms, soaked in a little boiling water
2 tablespoons olive oil
1 small onion, finely diced
1 garlic clove, crushed
110g (4oz) chestnut mushrooms, finely diced
250g (9oz) orzo
500ml (18fl oz) chicken stock
1 tablespoon lemon juice
1 tablespoon finely chopped fresh lemon thyme
50g (2oz) Parmesan, finely grated

Salad
1 bag of rocket leaves
4 tablespoons Parmesan shavings
2 tablespoons olive oil
2 tablespoons balsamic vinegar

Method

Chicken
Preheat the oven to 200°C/400°F/Gas 6 / Open the chicken breasts out, place each between 2 pieces of clingfilm and beat until 5mm (¼ inch) thick / Place a piece of pancetta on a board and lay a chicken breast across it / Place 3 basil leaves in the centre of the chicken, then top with 3 pieces of dolcelatte / In the gaps between the cheese, lay half a plum tomato / Season with salt and black pepper and roll up into a cylinder, securing with a cocktail stick if necessary / Make 3 more rolls the same way / Heat a frying pan, add the olive oil and the chicken rolls and cook for 1 minute on each side until golden / Put the rolls into a baking dish and place in the oven for 15–20 minutes, until sizzling and cooked through.

Orzo
While the chicken rolls are in the oven, drain the porcini mushrooms and chop finely / Heat a frying pan, add the olive oil and onion and cook for 1 minute / Add the garlic, porcini and chestnut mushrooms and cook for a further minute / Add the orzo and mix well / Add the stock, bring to a simmer, cover and cook for 5–8 minutes, until the liquid is absorbed and the orzo is tender / Remove the lid, add the lemon juice, lemon thyme and Parmesan and stir well / Season with salt and black pepper.

Salad
Toss the rocket leaves with the Parmesan, olive oil, vinegar, salt and black pepper.

To serve
Cut the chicken into thick slices / Pile some salad on each serving plate / Spoon the orzo alongside, and place the chicken on top.

Wine expert Olly Smith's choice
Tesco Finest Gavi
This is summer in a bottle, more melon than crisp green apple. It's got a fleshiness to it, and the savoury edge will pick up on the porcini and chestnut mushrooms.

Rachel Allen
Chicken and pilaf with green salad

This is a great, easy family dish, healthy, simple and fun. It will become a favourite in your house.

Ingredients Serves 6

Chicken
1 large chicken, about 2.5kg (5½lb), without giblets
1 carrot, halved
1 onion, halved
6 whole black peppercorns
1 large sprig of fresh parsley
1 large sprig of fresh thyme
725ml (1¼ pints) chicken stock
250ml (8fl oz) white wine
250 ml (8fl oz) single cream
50g (2oz) butter
50g (2oz) plain flour

Pilaf
25g (1oz) butter
1 small onion, chopped
300g (11oz) basmati rice
725ml (1¼ pints) vegetable (or chicken) stock

Dressing
3 tablespoons extra virgin olive oil
1 tablespoon white wine vinegar
1 teaspoon wholegrain mustard
1 teaspoon honey
1 large garlic clove, peeled and crushed
1 sprig of fresh parsley
A few fresh chives, chopped

Salad
A large selection of salad leaves, herbs and edible flowers, such as wild garlic, nasturtium, edible chrysanthemum and chives

Method

Chicken
Preheat the oven to 170°C/325°F/Gas 3 / Place the chicken in a large saucepan or casserole / Add the carrot, onion, peppercorns, herbs, stock and white wine and bring to the boil / Season with salt and black pepper, cover with the lid and place in the oven for 1½–2 hours, or until the chicken is completely cooked and the juices run clear when it is pierced (for a larger chicken, cook for 20 minutes per 450g (1lb) plus 30 minutes) / Remove the chicken from the stock and place it on a large plate / Remove all the meat from the carcass, discarding the skin and bones / Cut the chicken into strips approximately 1cm (½ inch) wide and 5cm (2 inches) long, cover and keep warm / Remove the vegetables, peppercorns and herbs from the liquid and discard / Add the cream, bring up to the boil and boil uncovered for a few minutes – if the flavour is a little weak, boil for longer, then season to taste / Heat a saucepan over a medium heat and melt the butter, then add the flour, continuing to stir on the heat / Allow it to cook for 2 minutes to form a roux / While the sauce is still boiling, whisk in the roux – you need enough to thicken it so it just about coats the back of a spoon / Place the chicken and any juices back in the casserole, once again correcting the seasoning.

Pilaf
About 30 minutes before the chicken is due to come out of the oven, melt the butter in a saucepan large enough to contain all the rice / Add the onion, cover and cook over a low heat for about 10 minutes, until the onion is soft / Add the rice and stir on the heat for about 2 minutes / Add the stock and some salt and black pepper, bring to the boil, then turn the heat right down to minimum and simmer for about 10 minutes, until the rice is just cooked and all the liquid has been absorbed.

Dressing and salad
Place all the dressing ingredients in a jar with a lid and shake to mix / Taste for seasoning / Wash and dry the salad leaves and flowers, tear them into bite-sized pieces and place them in a bowl.

To serve

Drizzle the dressing sparingly over the salad and toss gently / Pile the rice and salad on to serving plates and spoon the chicken alongside.

Wine expert Peter Richards's choice
Palestra Rueda Verdejo
The Verdejo grape variety from Rueda is often compared to Sauvignon Blanc. You get loads of really expressive herbal character on the nose, and on the palate it's really clean and citrusy, with a hint of spice. It's delicious.

Silvena Rowe

Pomegranate glazed duck with bulgar, chickpea and pomegranate pilaf

Pomegranate is a super food, and it helps make this dish a super supper!

Ingredients Serves 4

Duck

2 teaspoons pomegranate
  molasses
1 tablespoon runny honey
½ teaspoon caraway seeds,
  toasted and ground
4 duck breasts, skin scored
  diagonally

Pilaf

600ml (1 pint) strong
  vegetable stock
250g (9oz) coarse bulgar
  wheat
110g (4oz) tinned chickpeas
2–3 tablespoons extra virgin
  olive oil
2 red onions, sliced thinly
110g (4oz) dried sour cherries,
  roughly chopped
1 tablespoon pomegranate
  molasses
1 small bunch of fresh flat-leaf
  parsley, finely chopped
1 small bunch of fresh mint,
  finely chopped
110g (4oz) pistachio nuts,
  toasted and chopped
1 pomegranate, seeds only

Method

Duck

Preheat the oven to 200°C/400°F/Gas 6 / Mix together the pomegranate molasses, honey and caraway in a small bowl and rub this mixture on to the scored duck skin / Either allow to rest for an hour in the fridge or cook straight away / Heat a heavy non-stick pan, add the duck breasts, glazed skin side down, and cook for about a minute to brown and caramelise / Turn over and cook on the other side for 1 minute / Place in the oven for 8–11 minutes, until cooked to medium rare / Remove and set aside to rest for 5 minutes.

Pilaf

While the duck is cooking in the oven, place the vegetable stock in a saucepan and bring to the boil / Add the bulgar wheat and bring to a simmer / Reduce the heat and cook for 5–8 minutes until tender and all the liquid has been absorbed / Season with salt and black pepper, then add the chickpeas and mix well / Meanwhile, heat a heavy-based deep non-stick pan, add the olive oil and onions and cook for 3 minutes until soft / Add the sour cherries and pomegranate molasses, and cook for a further 3–5 minutes until the onions are caramelised and the cherries are plump / Add this mixture to the bulgar and mix well / Check the seasoning and add the chopped herbs, pistachios and pomegranate seeds.

To serve

Cut each duck breast into 2 and place on serving plates / Spoon the cooking juices over and scatter with a few pomegranate seeds / Pile the pilaf into a small bowl and serve alongside the duck.

Wine expert Susie Barrie's choice
Casa Mia Sangiovese
This wine is made purely from the Sangiovese grape. That gives it a wonderfully tangy sour cherry note that will be perfect with the pilaf and the pomegranate glaze on the duck.

James Martin
Spiced tadeek rice with Moroccan rice-coated chicken and preserved lemon salad

Cooking this authentic dish will transport you straight to the middle of a Marrakesh street market.

Ingredients Serves 4

Rice
300g (11oz) basmati rice
1 tablespoon olive oil
1 onion, finely chopped
1 garlic clove, finely chopped
½ teaspoon ground cinnamon
½ teaspoon sumac
50g (2oz) pistachios, roughly chopped
20g (¾oz) currants
4 tablespoons roughly chopped fresh flat-leaf parsley
50g (2oz) butter, melted
Large pinch of saffron, soaked in 2 tablespoons water
Juice of 1 lemon

Chicken
75g (3oz) basmati rice, soaked in water
3 teaspoons baharat spice (mixed Middle Eastern spices)
1 egg, beaten
4 chicken thighs, boneless and skinless, cut into strips
2 tablespoons olive oil

Salad
3 preserved lemons, deseeded and finely diced
4 tablespoons roughly chopped fresh flat-leaf parsley
2 tablespoons mint, roughly chopped
½ cucumber, deseeded and roughly chopped
Juice of ½ lemon
2 tablespoons extra virgin olive oil

Method

Rice
Bring a large pan of salted water to the boil, add the rice, cook for 4 minutes, then drain and refresh in cold water / Meanwhile, heat a frying pan, add the oil, onion and garlic and cook for 2 minutes / Add the cinnamon, sumac, pistachios, currants and parsley and mix well / Put the melted butter into a medium saucepan and sprinkle over enough cooked rice to cover the bottom / Add the onion mixture to the remaining rice and mix well / Add the saffron and its soaking liquid, lemon juice, salt and black pepper and stir gently / Spoon into the saucepan, piling the rice up slightly towards the centre / Cover with a damp tea towel, followed by a tight-fitting lid / Place on a very low heat and cook for 25–30 minutes, until the rice is tender and a golden crust has formed on the bottom – take care to keep the heat very low, as it will burn very easily.

Chicken
Meanwhile, put the soaked rice into a frying pan and place on the heat / Cook for 1–2 minutes, until just golden / Remove to a pestle and mortar, add the baharat spice and crush to a powder / Put the beaten egg and the spice mixture into 2 separate shallow bowls / Season the chicken strips with salt and black pepper and then toss first into the beaten egg and then into the spices, making sure all are thoroughly coated / Heat a frying pan and add the olive oil and chicken / Cook for 2–3 minutes each side, until golden and cooked through.

Salad
Toss all the ingredients together in a bowl and season with a little salt and black pepper.

To serve

Lift the lid and tea towel from the rice / Place a plate over the top and invert to tip the rice out / The crusty base should come out with the rice – if it doesn't, put the base of the saucepan into a bowl of cold water, which should help loosen the crust / Spoon the rice on to serving plates, adding a few of the crusty pieces from the bottom of the pan / Place the chicken alongside, with a spoonful of salad.

Wine expert Peter Richards's choice
Sainsbury's Taste the Difference Gewürztraminer

Ken Hom
Garlic chicken with cucumber and spicy Sichuan noodles

The Chinese believe that long noodles represent a long life, so cut them at your peril!

Ingredients Serves 4

Chicken
450g (1lb) cucumber, peeled and halved lengthways
2 tablespoons salt
1 tablespoon groundnut oil
450g (1lb) chicken breasts, boneless and skinless, cut into 2.5cm (1 inch) cubes
1½ tablespoons crushed garlic
1 tablespoon finely chopped spring onions
1 tablespoon light soy sauce
1 tablespoon Shaoxing rice wine or dry sherry
2 teaspoons chilli bean sauce, or chilli powder
2 teaspoons sesame oil

Noodles
225g (8oz) minced fatty pork
3 tablespoons dark soy sauce
2 teaspoons Shaoxing rice wine or dry sherry
1 teaspoon salt
½ teaspoon freshly ground black pepper
450g (1lb) fresh or dried Chinese egg noodles
2 tablespoons groundnut oil
2 tablespoons chilli oil
2 tablespoons crushed garlic
2 tablespoons grated fresh root ginger
5 tablespoons finely chopped spring onions
2 tablespoons sesame paste
2 teaspoons light soy sauce
2 teaspoons chilli bean sauce
250ml (8fl oz) chicken stock

To serve
2 teaspoons Sichuan peppercorns, roasted and ground

Method

Chicken
Remove the seeds from the cucumber with a teaspoon / Cut the cucumber into 2.5cm (1 inch) cubes, sprinkle with the salt and place in a colander to drain for 20 minutes / Rinse the cucumber cubes in cold running water and blot them dry with kitchen paper / Heat a wok or large frying pan over a high heat, add the oil, and when it is very hot and slightly smoking, add the chicken and stir-fry for a few seconds / Add all the other ingredients except the cucumber and continue to stir-fry for a further 2 minutes / Add the cucumber and keep stir-frying for 3 minutes more, then set aside and keep warm.

Noodles
While the salted cucumber is draining, mix together in a bowl the pork, 1 tablespoon dark soy sauce, rice wine, salt and pepper / Leave to marinate for 10 minutes / Cook the noodles according to the packet instructions, then plunge them into cold water, drain them thoroughly, toss them in the groundnut oil and put them aside until you are ready to use them – they can be kept in this state, tightly covered with clingfilm, for up to 2 hours in the fridge / When the chicken is cooked, heat a second wok or large frying pan over a high heat, add the chilli oil, and when it is very hot and slightly smoking, add the garlic, ginger and spring onions and stir-fry for 30 seconds / Add the pork and continue to stir-fry until it loses its pink colour / Add the rest of the noodle ingredients, including the remaining 2 tablespoons of dark soy sauce, and cook for a further 2 minutes / Now add the noodles, mixing well.

To serve
Turn the noodles out on to serving plates, spoon the chicken alongside and garnish with the Sichuan peppercorns.

Wine expert Susy Atkins's choice
Tim Adams Clare Valley Riesling
Premium Australian Riesling goes really well with Chinese food. What you get here is that lovely lemon and lime fruit, very clean, very zesty, but with a roundness as well to go with the pork and ginger.

Paul Rankin
Spiced chicken livers with Chinese noodles, soy, black pepper and cream

The clever tip of soaking the livers in milk takes away the risk of any bitterness.

Ingredients Serves 4

Chicken livers

350g (12oz) fresh chicken
  livers, trimmed and cut
  in half
150ml (5fl oz) milk
2 tablespoons vegetable oil
1 tablespoon butter
2 teaspoons grated fresh root
  ginger
1 teaspoon soft brown sugar
1 teaspoon cracked black
  peppercorns
4 tablespoons Japanese soy
  sauce
2 tablespoons dry sherry
100ml (3½fl oz) double cream
2 tablespoons chopped fresh
  coriander

Noodles

1 packet of dried Chinese egg
  noodles (approx 200g/7oz)

Method

Chicken livers

Put the livers into a bowl with the milk and some ice, place in the fridge and allow to soak for at least 1 hour / Drain the livers and pat them dry / Heat a large frying pan over a high heat, and season the livers with salt and black pepper / Add the vegetable oil and butter to the pan, and heat until the butter is foaming / Add the chicken livers and fry for about 2 minutes on each side – don't stir them around too much, which will allow them to turn brown / Add the ginger and fry for 30 seconds more / Add the sugar, pepper, soy sauce and sherry and cook until reduced enough to give the livers just a light glaze / Remove the livers with a slotted spoon to a plate and keep warm / Add the cream and fresh coriander to the pan and boil until the cream thickens a little.

Noodles

Meanwhile, cook the noodles according to the packet instructions.

To serve

Place a pile of noodles on each serving plate, top with the livers and pour over the sauce.

Wine expert Susie Barrie's choice

Sainsbury's Taste the Difference 12 Year Old Dry Amontillado Sherry
If you get a proper dry sherry that's made by a good producer and you match it with the right type of food, it can taste absolutely fantastic. This one is amazing, the taste just lingers and lingers.

Nic Watt
Grilled poussin marinated in ume shu and miso with a pickle salad

This will work just as well using a chicken breast. You can buy the ume shu plums in plum wine – a cheaper way to buy both ingredients.

Ingredients Serves 4

Pickle salad
150ml (5fl oz) white wine vinegar
90ml (3½fl oz) mirin
50g (2oz) caster sugar
Pinch of salt
12 Thai shallots, thinly sliced
75g (3oz) edamame beans, blanched
6 tablespoons fresh coriander leaves, torn
3 tablespoons fresh mint leaves, torn
2 green chillies, deseeded and finely sliced

Poussin
2 x 500g (1lb 2oz) poussin
1 tablespoon grated fresh root ginger
2 garlic cloves
1 tablespoon finely chopped shallot
1 spring onion, roughly chopped
2 tablespoons plum wine
110ml (4fl oz) yaki niku barbecue sauce
2 teaspoons teriyaki sauce
½ teaspoon ao nori
25ml (1fl oz) olive oil
75g (3oz) mugi miso
4 ume shu plums, from the plum wine

Method

Pickle salad
Place the vinegar, mirin, sugar and salt in a saucepan and bring to the boil / Simmer for 2 minutes until the sugar is dissolved, then pour into a bowl / Put the Thai shallots into the hot pickle liquid and leave for 2 hours at room temperature / Remove the shallots from the bowl, reserving the liquid / Place the pickled shallots, edamame beans, torn coriander and mint leaves and sliced green chilli in a bowl / Toss with 2 tablespoons of the cooled pickle liquid and set aside.

Poussin
Meanwhile quarter the poussin, leaving in the breast and thigh bones / Place all the remaining poussin ingredients, except the plums, into a food processor and blend to a smooth marinade / Remove the stones from the plums, then roughly chop and add to the marinade / Spoon the marinade over the poussin and place in the fridge for 1 hour / When ready to cook, heat the grill to high / Heat a griddle pan, add the poussin pieces, skin side down, and cook for 2 minutes / Turn and cook for a further 2 minutes / Place the poussin on a parchment-lined grill tray and baste with the remaining marinade / Place under the grill and cook for about 10 minutes, basting 2 or 3 times with the marinade, until cooked through and caramelised.

To serve
Arrange the grilled poussin on serving plates and top neatly with the pickle salad.

Wine expert Peter Richards's choice
Leitz Riesling Kabinett
What German Riesling does brilliantly is give you intensity with sweetness, but it also gives you a lovely delicacy of flavour. That's exactly what we want with Nic's dish, and this one's superb.

Daniel Galmiche
Pan-roasted chicken breast with leeks and potatoes

The addition of truffles to this simple recipe turns an ordinary chicken breast into a spectacular dish. You can freeze the truffles if you have any left over.

Ingredients Serves 2

Chicken
2 chicken breasts, wing on and skin on
2 small winter truffles (white or black), thinly sliced

Leeks and potatoes
2–3 small leeks, thinly sliced
200g (7oz) small new potatoes, sliced 5mm (¼ inch) thick
200g (7oz) pancetta, thinly sliced
1 tablespoon olive oil
2 sprigs of fresh chervil
50g (2oz) butter

Method

Chicken
Preheat the oven to 190°C/375°F/Gas 5 / Slit the skin of the chicken breasts and place 3 thin slices of truffle underneath / Fold the skin back over the chicken and season both sides of the chicken with salt and black pepper / Cut the remaining truffle slices into thin julienne strips and set aside for the vegetables / Heat a frying pan, add the chicken, skin side down, and cook for 2–3 minutes, until golden – make sure the pan is not too hot so that the skin does not shrink back too much / Turn the chicken over and cook for a further minute, then place in the oven for 8 minutes / Remove the chicken breasts from the oven and place on a plate to rest.

Leeks and potatoes
While the chicken is in the oven, heat a pan of salted water until boiling, drop in the leeks and cook for 1 minute / Drain, refresh in iced water and drain once more / Put the potatoes and pancetta together into a pan of boiling water, cook for 1 minute, then drain, refresh in iced water and drain again / Heat a frying pan, add the olive oil, potatoes and pancetta and cook for 1–2 minutes, until golden brown / Add the green part of the leeks and some of the truffle julienne to the pan, along with the chervil / Drain any fat from the frying pan, add 2–3 tablespoons of water and stir to make a sauce / Add the butter and the remaining truffle julienne and cook until the butter has melted.

To serve
Cut each chicken breast into 3 pieces / Place some of the leek and potato mixture in the middle of each serving plate, put the chicken on top, and pour over the truffle butter sauce.

Wine expert Peter Richards's choice
Gran Sasso Pecorino
Pecorino is an ancient, almost forgotten grape variety, but it's being revived. With this wine you get lovely herbal and dried fruit aromas on the nose and it has a delicious salty tang to it, which will match up brilliantly with the truffles.

Raymond Blanc
Poached chicken wih a fricassée of wild mushrooms

A French classic from a classic French chef!

Ingredients Serves 2

Persillade
½ garlic clove, crushed
1 teaspoon finely chopped
  shallot
Handful of fresh flat-leaf
  parsley, roughly chopped

Chicken
125ml (4½fl oz) water
20g (¾oz) butter
30g (1¼oz) carrot, cut in half
  lengthways then into 5mm
  (¼ inch) slices
30g (1¼oz) celery, cut into
  5mm (¼ inch) slices
30g (1¼oz) leek, cut into 5mm
  (¼ inch) rings
30g (1¼oz) courgette, cut in
  half lengthways then cut
  into 5mm (¼ inch) slices
1 sprig of fresh tarragon
2 x 200g (7oz) chicken
  breasts, boneless and
  skinless
50g (2oz) girolles or pied
  de mouton mushrooms,
  trimmed
50g (2oz) button mushrooms,
  quartered
50g (2oz) chanterelles,
  trimmed
30g (1¼oz) trompettes,
  trimmed and split in two
40g (1½oz) tomatoes,
  deseeded and cut into 1cm
  (½ inch) dice

Method

Persillade
Mix the garlic, shallot and parsley together in a small bowl and set aside.

Chicken
In a medium sauté pan on a high heat, bring the water and butter to the boil, then add the carrot, celery, leeks, courgettes and tarragon / Season the chicken breasts with salt and freshly ground black pepper and place in the pan on top of the vegetables / Cover with a lid and simmer for 5 minutes / Add all the mushrooms apart from the trompettes, replace the lid and cook for a further minute / Stir in the trompettes and continue to cook for 30 seconds / Add the diced tomato and the persillade / Taste and adjust the seasoning if necessary.

To serve

Remove the chicken from the pan and cut in half / Spoon a little of the vegetables on to each serving plate / Top with the chicken, a further spoonful of vegetables and some cooking juices.

Wine expert Tim Atkin's choice
Baron de Ley Rioja Reserva
This dish would work equally well with a white or a red wine. This is a lighter style of red with a little bit of oak flavour in it, which will go quite nicely with the earthiness of the mushrooms.

Patrick Williams
Jerk Kiev with yam forestière

The jerk seasoning gives the classic Kiev an interesting twist and a kick! Use ordinary breadcrumbs if you can't find Japanese ones.

Ingredients Serves 4

Chicken

4 x 200g (7oz) chicken breast, skinless, with the wing bone retained
1 tablespoon olive oil
2 tablespoons jerk seasoning paste
3 garlic cloves, crushed
200g (7oz) butter, softened
2 shallots, finely diced
2 tablespoons finely chopped fresh curly parsley
Juice of ½ lime
4 eggs, beaten
110ml (4fl oz) milk
110g (4oz) plain flour
500g (1lb 2oz) Japanese breadcrumbs

Yam

500g (1lb 2oz) yellow or white yam, peeled and cut into 1cm (½ inch) chunks
4 tablespoons olive oil
4 rashers smoked streaky bacon, roughly chopped
110g (4oz) wild mushrooms

Method

Chicken

Make an incision in the top of each chicken breast, then wiggle the knife around to create a pocket and set aside / Heat a frying pan, add the olive oil, jerk paste and garlic and cook for 1 minute / Put the butter into a bowl, add the cooked jerk paste and garlic, shallots, parsley and lime juice and beat together / Season with salt and black pepper / Place into a piping bag and pipe into the pockets you made in the chicken / Place in the fridge until the butter inside the chicken is just set – about 30 minutes / Heat a deep-fat fryer to 190°C, and the oven to 200°C/400°F/Gas 6 / Beat the eggs and milk together / Put the flour, beaten eggs and breadcrumbs into 3 separate shallow bowls / Dip the chicken breasts first into the flour, then into the eggs and finally into the breadcrumbs, making sure both sides are totally covered / Place the chicken in the deep-fat fryer and cook for 2 minutes, until golden brown / Remove and place on a roasting tray in the oven for 5–8 minutes, until cooked through.

Yam

Meanwhile, bring a pan of salted water to the boil / Add the yams and simmer for 2–3 minutes, until just tender, then drain and set aside / Heat a frying pan, add the olive oil and the yams and fry until golden brown all over / Heat a second frying pan, add the bacon and cook for 1 minute / Add the mushrooms and sauté for 2–3 minutes, until cooked through / Add the yams to the bacon and mushrooms and toss to combine / Season with salt and black pepper.

To serve

Spoon the yam mixture into the centre of each serving plate / Cut the chicken in half on the diagonal and place on top.

Wine expert Susy Atkins's choice
Cave de Beblenheim Pinot Gris
Today, white wines tend to fall into two categories: heavy, very oaky and rather rich styles, or super-crisp, bone-dry wines. This is a rare example of one that falls between the two and hits a fine balance.

Theo Randall
Boned chicken stuffed with prosciutto, mascarpone and rosemary, served with purple sprouting and romanesco broccoli

Try to find these broccoli varieties as they give the dish a real wow factor.

Ingredients Serves 2

Stuffed chicken
1 x 1.2–1.5kg (2lb 9oz–3lb 4oz) chicken, boned, with the exception of the wing
4 slices of prosciutto
150g (5oz) mascarpone
2 sprigs of fresh rosemary, finely chopped
Zest and juice of 1½ lemons
2 tablespoons olive oil

Broccoli
150g (5oz) purple sprouting broccoli, trimmed
150g (5oz) romanesco broccoli, cut into spears
2 tablespoons olive oil

Method

Stuffed chicken
Preheat the oven to 200°C/400°F/Gas 6 / Lay the chicken on a board, skin side down / Remove the 2 mini fillets of chicken breast and set aside / Lay the prosciutto over the remaining chicken breast and push into the leg cavities / Mix the mascarpone with the rosemary, lemon zest and juice in a small bowl / Place a spoonful of mascarpone on both breasts and in the leg cavities, reserving 1 spoonful / Flatten the mini fillets slightly and replace on top of the mascarpone-covered breasts / Roll the chicken over, tucking the legs back under and the skin around to form a chicken-like shape / Heat an ovenproof frying pan and add the olive oil / Season the chicken and place skin side down in the frying pan for 2 minutes, or until the skin is golden / Place in the oven for 15–18 minutes, until cooked through / Remove the chicken from the oven and drain any excess fat from the pan, leaving the meat juices / Place the chicken on a plate and set aside to rest for 5 minutes / Add the last spoonful of mascarpone to the pan and whisk into the juices to make a sauce.

Broccoli
When the chicken is almost ready, bring a large pan of salted water to the boil / Add the purple sprouting broccoli and the romanesco and cook for 3 minutes, until just tender, and drain / Put back into the pan, toss with the olive oil and season with salt and black pepper.

To serve

Cut the chicken in half and serve with the broccoli and the mascarpone sauce.

Wine expert Tim Atkin's choice
Paul Mas Estate Marsanne Vin de Pays d'Oc
This is a French red with a Mediterranean twist, and it's absolutely wonderful. On the nose it's got lovely aromas – honeysuckle, a bit of lemon in there, some pear, with just an undertone of tropical fruit.

James Martin
Chorizo chicken with sautéd chorizo, potatoes and spinach

This easy dish is a great way to use chorizo, which is readily available in most supermarkets.

Ingredients Serves 4

Chicken
4 x 175g (6oz) chicken breasts, boneless and skinless
4 teaspoons olive oil
1 banana shallot, finely diced
175g (6oz) cured chorizo, cut into small dice
2 tablespoons roughly chopped fresh flat-leaf parsley
Zest of 1 lemon

Chorizo and potatoes
300g (11oz) semi-cured chorizo, cut into chunks
450g (1lb) cooked new potatoes, cut into quarters
250g (9oz) cherry tomatoes, cut in half
3 tablespoons roughly chopped fresh flat-leaf parsley

Spinach
50g (2oz) butter
600g (1lb 5oz) baby leaf spinach

Method

Chicken
Preheat the oven to 200°C/400°F/Gas 6 / Make a slit in the side of each chicken breast and press the knife in and around, to create a pocket / Season the chicken with salt and black pepper / Heat a frying pan, add 2 teaspoons of olive oil and the shallot and cook for 1 minute, until just softened / Remove from the heat and place in a bowl, along with the chorizo, parsley and lemon zest / Toss together and season with a little black pepper / Open the side of each chicken breast and press the chorizo mixture into the pocket, filling them as full as possible / Heat a frying pan, add the remaining olive oil and the chicken breasts and fry on each side for 1–2 minutes, until golden brown / Place in the oven for 15–18 minutes, until cooked through / Remove from the oven and set aside to rest for a few minutes.

Chorizo and potatoes
While the chicken is resting, heat a frying pan, add the chorizo and cook for a couple of minutes, until the oil starts to come out / Add the potatoes, and fry until golden and crispy / Add the tomatoes and fry for a further 2 minutes until just softened / Add the parsley, salt and black pepper and toss well.

Spinach
When the potatoes are nearly ready, heat a large pan, add the butter and spinach and cook until just wilted / Season with salt and black pepper.

To serve
Place a pile of spinach in the centre of each serving plate / Carve the chicken breasts diagonally into 3 and place on top / Spoon the sautéd chorizo and potatoes around the side and top with any oily chorizo juices.

Wine expert Olly Smith's choice
Marqués de Cáceres Rioja Blanco

Si King
Festive duck breast with pancetta, Savoy cabbage and mash

This is a great alternative at Christmas but equally it makes a great show dish all year round.

Ingredients Serves 2

Duck
2 duck breasts, skin on
2 star anise
1 cinnamon stick
2 cloves
Zest of ½ orange
150ml (5fl oz) port
110ml (4fl oz) chicken stock
25g (1oz) butter
4 slices of black pudding
1 pear, peeled and cut into
   wedges

Mash
500g (1lb 2oz) King Edward
   potatoes, peeled and cut
   into chunks
50g (2oz) butter
75ml (3fl oz) milk

Cabbage
110g (4oz) pancetta, cut into
   small cubes
2 tablespoons maple syrup
½ Savoy cabbage, finely
   shredded

Method

Duck
Score a diamond pattern across the duck skin and season both sides of the breasts with salt and black pepper / Heat a frying pan and add the duck breasts, skin side down / Turn the heat down to low and cook for 6 minutes on each side for pink, 8 minutes on each side for well done / Remove from the pan and set aside to rest on a plate / Pour off most of the duck fat from the pan and turn up the heat / Add the star anise, cinnamon, cloves and orange zest and fry for 1 minute / Add the port and bring to a simmer, stirring to release the duck juices from the bottom of the pan / Add the stock and cook for 3 minutes over a high heat, reducing and thickening the sauce / Season with salt and black pepper / Heat a separate frying pan, add the butter, black pudding and pears and fry for 1–2 minutes on each side, until golden brown.

Mash
While the duck is cooking, place the potatoes in a saucepan, cover with water and add a pinch of salt / Bring to the boil and cook for 15–18 minutes, until tender / Drain the potatoes and return them to the pan over the heat to drive off any excess moisture / Mash well, then add the butter and milk and season to taste.

Cabbage
When the duck is nearly cooked, heat a frying pan, add the pancetta and cook for 2 minutes, until golden brown and all the fat has been released / Add the maple syrup and toss to coat / Add the cabbage and toss once more, then cook for 2–3 minutes to wilt down / Season with a little salt and plenty of black pepper.

To serve

Carve the duck in thick diagonal slices / Spoon the mash on to serving plates and top with the duck / Spoon a pile of cabbage, the black pudding and pear wedges alongside / Spoon the sauce over the duck.

Wine expert Olly Smith's choice
Villa Maria Cellar Selection Pinot Noir
Pinot Noir and duck is a marriage made in heaven. This has a lovely zip that will work with the freshness of those pears, and a richness, a brambly quality, that will work fantastically with the black pudding.

Jun Tanaka
Salt crust chicken with peas, broad beans and mousseron mushrooms

The salt crust in this stunning dish keeps the chicken lovely and moist.

Ingredients Serves 2

Salt crust
250g (9oz) coarse sea salt
4 tablespoons chopped
    fresh thyme
2 tablespoons chopped
    fresh rosemary
2 eggs
50ml (2fl oz) water
200g (7oz) pasta flour

Chicken
1.6kg (3lb 8oz) chicken, legs
    and wings removed
1 sprig of fresh rosemary
1 sprig of fresh thyme
1 head of garlic
½ lemon
15g (½oz) butter

Sauce
15g (½oz) butter
1 shallot, finely chopped
75g (3oz) fresh peas, podded
75g (3oz) fresh broad beans,
    podded and skinned
50g (2oz) mousseron
    mushrooms (or other wild
    mushrooms)
110ml (4fl oz) Sauternes wine
50ml (2fl oz) Chardonnay
    vinegar
175ml (6fl oz) chicken stock
1 tablespoon crème fraîche
2 tablespoons roughly
    chopped fresh chervil

Method

Salt crust
Mix together the salt, herbs, eggs and water in a bowl / Slowly work in the flour until you have a firm, elastic dough / Wrap the dough in clingfilm and leave to rest for 1 hour / On a lightly floured surface, roll the dough out to about 5mm (¼ inch) in thickness – it should be around 30 x 25cm (12 x 10 inches).

Chicken
Meanwhile, preheat the oven to 220°C/425°F/Gas 7 / Stuff the cavity of the chicken with the sprigs of rosemary and thyme, the garlic head and the lemon half / Season the chicken with black pepper, then place in the centre of the salt crust dough, breast side down, and wrap completely in the dough / Turn over so the seam is on the bottom, and place on a baking tray / Place in the oven for 25 minutes / Remove and set aside to rest for a further 25 minutes / Crack open the salt crust, wipe the chicken with a clean cloth and remove both breasts from the carcass / Heat a frying pan, add the butter and fry the chicken breasts, skin side down, until golden and heated through.

Sauce
While the chicken is resting, heat a frying pan, add the butter and shallot and cook for 1 minute / Add the peas, broad beans and mousserons and cook for 2 minutes / Pour in the wine and vinegar and cook until reduced by two-thirds / Add the stock and reduce by half / Add the crème fraîche, season with salt and black pepper and stir in the chopped chervil.

To serve

Spoon the pea mixture on to serving plates and top with a chicken breast.

Wine expert Olly Smith's choice
Les Quatre Clochers Chardonnay
This wine is all about freshness and has a dazzling quality. It has a fantastic aroma, with just a subtle use of oak that's going to go marvellously with the mushrooms.

Daniel Galmiche
Lemon chicken casserole

Ooh la la! This is the perfect one-pot casserole.

Ingredients Serves 4

Chicken
2 tablespoons honey
2 lemons
2kg (4lb 4oz) chicken, cut into
    8 pieces
60g (2½ oz) butter
1 tablespoon olive oil
4 unpeeled garlic cloves,
    lightly crushed
500ml (18fl oz) chicken stock
2 sprigs of fresh thyme

Spinach
60g (2½ oz) butter
250g (9oz) baby leaf spinach

Method

Chicken
Preheat the oven to 200°C/400°F/Gas 6 / Place the honey in a large bowl with the zest and juice of 1 lemon and a little salt / Whisk together, then add the chicken, season with black pepper and toss / Heat a heatproof casserole dish and add half of the butter, half the olive oil and half the chicken / Fry until golden brown, then set aside / Repeat with the remaining butter, oil and chicken / Slice the remaining lemon thinly / Add the garlic cloves, lemon slices and remaining honey marinade to the pan and deglaze / Put the chicken back into the pan and add the stock and thyme / Bring to the boil, then place in the oven for 30–35 minutes / When cooked, remove the chicken from the casserole and set aside to keep warm / Return the casserole to the heat, bring the sauce to the boil, and cook until it has the consistency of a light syrup / Strain into a saucepan, pressing the garlic through a sieve, and season with salt and black pepper.

Spinach
Heat a large frying pan, add the butter and spinach and cook until just wilted.

To serve

Place some spinach in the centre of each serving plate / Top with 2 pieces of chicken, and spoon the sauce over the top.

Wine expert Peter Richards's choice
Dourthe La Grande Cuvée Sauvignon Blanc
This wine is vibrant, fresh and aromatic. It's tangy and persistent, and that's going to accentuate the citrus elements of the dish and is even going to pick up well on the honey.

Rump steak teriyaki with a salad of radish, pea shoots and mustard

Beef koftas with grilled fig and halloumi salad

Beef tagliata

Beef flank, crispy shallot, wild mushroom and watercress salad

Sirloin steaks in a tomato and caper sauce

Beef rendang with lemongrass and ginger, Thai herb salad and sticky rice

Chilli beef with spicy noodles

Thai red penang curry

Beef fillet with coconut milk served with baby gems, crispy noodles and dipping sauce

Braised oxtail and beetroot with creamy mash

La gran lasagna

Bourbon glazed sticky ribs with coleslaw and baked potato

Aztec's molcajete

Slow-cooked beef with horseradish mash, mushroom tortellini, buttered cabbage and red wine sauce

Pan-fried veal fillet with wild mushrooms, asparagus, wild garlic and a sherry sauce

Veal chops with spätzle

Griddled veal rump with roasted ceps and mixed leaf and walnut salad

Beef & Veal

Paul Rankin
Rump steak teriyaki with a salad of radish, pea shoots and mustard

This is a lovely take on a summer steak salad. The mustard is traditional, but the pea shoots and radish give a hot modern twist.

Ingredients Serves 4

Steak
4 x 175g (6oz) 28-day aged rump steaks, cut about 2cm (¾ inch) thick
3 tablespoons mirin
3 tablespoons Japanese soy sauce
3 tablespoons sake
2 tablespoons vegetable oil

Salad
¼ small red onion, finely sliced, soaked in iced water for 15 minutes
110g (4oz) mooli radish, cut or peeled into thin strips
6 red radishes, finely sliced
Handful of pea shoots (or watercress)
4 tablespoons fresh peas, blanched

Dressing
2 teaspoons English mustard
1 teaspoon wholegrain mustard
½ teaspoon caster sugar
1 teaspoon wine vinegar
1 tablespoon rapeseed oil
1–2 tablespoons water

Method

Steak
Season the steaks with salt and black pepper / Whisk the mirin, soy sauce and sake together in a bowl to make the teriyaki sauce / Heat a frying pan, add the oil and the steaks and cook on each side for 2–3 minutes, then remove from the pan and set aside to rest / Pour off any fat from the frying pan, then add the teriyaki sauce / Bring to the boil and simmer for a couple of minutes until thickened and shiny / Return the steaks to the frying pan, spoon over the sauce and cook for a further minute until nicely glazed.

Salad and dressing
While the steaks are cooking, toss all the salad ingredients together in a bowl / Next, whisk all the dressing ingredients together in a bowl.

To serve

Cut the steak into thick slices and place on serving plates / Add some salad to each plate, and drizzle with a little of the mustard dressing.

Wine expert Peter Richards's choice
Trivento Reserve Shiraz/Malbec
This is a juicier, fresher style of red without too much oak or tannin. You get enough body and richness and a wonderful peppery, spicy lift from this Malbec.

James Martin
Beef koftas with grilled fig and halloumi salad

These are great either on a barbecue or on the griddle. If you're using wooden skewers, don't forget to pre-soak them otherwise they'll burn.

Ingredients Serves 4

Koftas
475g (1Ib 1oz) beef mince
1 garlic clove, crushed
½ teaspoon ground coriander
1 teaspoon ground cumin

Salad
4 figs, thickly sliced
200g (7oz) halloumi, thickly sliced
1 bunch of salad leaves

Dressing
Juice of ½ lemon
3 tablespoons extra virgin olive oil

Method

Koftas
Soak 8 small wooden skewers in cold water / Put the beef mince into a bowl with the garlic, coriander, cumin, and some salt and black pepper / Mix well and divide into 8 / Press one of the beef portions around a skewer forming a sausage, three-quarters the length of the skewer / Repeat with the remaining meat and skewers, then place in the fridge to firm up / Heat a griddle pan until hot, then add the skewers and cook for 2–3 minutes on each side.

Salad and dressing
When the koftas are nearly ready, heat a frying pan until hot, add the fig slices and fry on each side for 30 seconds / Remove the figs from the pan, then add the halloumi and cook on each side for 1 minute / Wash and dry the salad leaves and put them into a bowl / Whisk the dressing ingredients together and season with salt and black pepper.

To serve

Drizzle most of the dressing over the salad leaves / Arrange alternate slices of fig and halloumi in the centre of each serving plate / Place a pile of salad leaves on top and finish with 2 koftas / Drizzle over the remaining dressing.

Sarah Raven
Beef tagliata

Sarah grows all her own vegetables and brought them in when she cooked this dish on the show. Use the freshest you can get hold of, preferably home-grown. You can improvise with the leaves, but they need to be peppery.

Ingredients Serves 8

Beef

3 garlic cloves, roughly chopped
1 red chilli, deseeded and roughly chopped
300ml (11fl oz) soy sauce
110ml (4fl oz) sunflower oil
1.35kg (3lb) beef fillet, trimmed

Dressing

6 tablespoons soy sauce
1 heaped tablespoon finely chopped fresh root ginger
1 fresh red chilli, deseeded and finely chopped
2 garlic cloves, finely chopped
Juice of ½ lemon
1 tablespoon Thai fish sauce
1 tablespoon soft light brown sugar

Salad

3 or 4 large handfuls of mixed peppery winter leaves, such as rocket, Golden Streaks mustard, Mustard 'Osaka Purple', Treviso, chicory 'Variegata del Castelfranco'
4 tablespoons roughly chopped fresh coriander leaves

Method

Beef

Place the garlic, chilli, soy sauce and sunflower oil in a blender and process until smooth / Spread over the beef fillet and leave for several hours or overnight, turning from time to time / When ready to cook the beef, preheat the oven to 220°C/425°F/Gas 7 and bring the fillet to room temperature / Heat a frying pan until hot, then seal the beef on each side until brown / Transfer to a roasting tin, place in the oven and cook for 20 minutes, then remove from the oven and set aside to cool.

Dressing and salad

While the beef is cooking, put all the dressing ingredients into a bowl and whisk to combine / Wash the salad leaves, refresh in cold water, then dry the leaves and mix together in a bowl.

To serve

Arrange the salad leaves on serving plates / Thinly slice the beef fillet and arrange it over the leaves / Drizzle with the dressing.

Wine expert Susie Barrie's choice
St Hallett Gamekeeper's Reserve

This is a blended variety that isn't oaked. It's a light, fruity style of wine, which is what we need with this dish because wines with too much tannin and oak don't really work with spicy food.

Mark Hix
Beef flank, crispy shallot, wild mushroom and watercress salad

Flank of beef is a bit tougher than fillet, but this cheaper, lesser-used cut is way ahead in the flavour stakes.

Ingredients Serves 4

Beef
2 x 300g (10oz) flank or
  hanger steaks
110g (4oz) plain flour
5–6 shallots, peeled and sliced
  into thin rings
110ml (4fl oz) milk
2 tablespoons olive oil
150g (5oz) mixed wild
  mushrooms

Dressing
1 tablespoon good quality
  cider vinegar
3 tablespoons extra virgin
  olive oil
1 teaspoon English mustard

Salad
110–150g (4–5oz) watercress,
  trimmed and thick stalks
  removed

Method

Beef
Trim the steaks of any excess fat and set them aside at room temperature / Put about 7.5cm (3 inches) of oil into an electric deep-fat fryer or a heavy-based frying pan and heat to 160–180°C / Season the flour generously with salt and pepper / Toss the shallot rings in the seasoned flour to coat, shaking off any excess, then dip into the milk and then into the flour again, shaking off the excess / Deep-fry the shallot rings a handful at a time for 3–4 minutes, until crisp, then remove with a slotted spoon and drain on kitchen paper / Heat a ridged griddle pan or a heavy-based frying pan (or better still a barbecue) / Season the steaks well and cook to your liking – allow about 3–4 minutes on each side for rare to medium rare (which I'd recommend for a salad) / Heat a frying pan, add the olive oil and mushrooms and sauté for 2–3 minutes, until softened and just coloured.

Dressing and salad
While the steaks are cooking, whisk the dressing ingredients together in a bowl and season with salt and pepper to taste.

To serve

Arrange the watercress on serving plates and drizzle with the dressing / Slice the steaks, arrange on top of the watercress, and scatter the wild mushrooms and shallots on top.

Wine expert Susy Atkins's choice
De Forville Dolcetto d'Alba
This wine is extremely food-friendly. It has a nice rich, dark colour and a kind of pepperiness on the palate. At its core is that lovely, soft, moreish cherry fruit, which will go so well with the beef.

Gennaro Contaldo
Sirloin steaks in a tomato and caper sauce

With his simple yet brilliant twists on classic Italian dishes like this, you can understand why Gennaro is such an inspiration to Jamie Oliver.

Ingredients Serves 4

Steak
4 x 150g (6oz) sirloin steaks, thinly cut
3 tablespoons olive oil

Sauce
2 garlic cloves, thinly sliced
6 anchovy fillets
2 tablespoons capers, rinsed and dried
Handful of fresh flat-leaf parsley, finely chopped
400g (14oz) tinned plum tomatoes
2 tablespoons dried oregano

Couscous
200g (7oz) couscous
1 red pepper, finely diced
1 large shallot, finely diced
Juice of 1 lemon
2 tablespoons olive oil
3 tablespoons chopped fresh flat-leaf parsley

Method

Steak
Heat a frying pan, add the olive oil and steaks and fry on each side until browned / Remove the steaks and set aside on a plate.

Sauce
Add the garlic, anchovies, capers and half the parsley to the pan you browned the steaks in, and fry for 2–3 minutes / Add the tomatoes and oregano and cook for 1 minute on a high heat, stirring well / Reduce the heat, add the steaks and any juices from the plate and make sure they are covered with the sauce / Simmer for 10–15 minutes.

Couscous
While the sauce is cooking, place the couscous in a bowl and pour over enough boiling water to cover by 1cm (½ inch) / Stir well, then cover with clingfilm and leave for 3–5 minutes / Remove the clingfilm and stir the couscous well with a fork / Add the remaining ingredients and mix well.

To serve

Pile the couscous on to serving plates, lay the steak on top and spoon over the sauce.

Wine expert Olly Smith's choice
Tesco's Finest Nero d'Avola
If you're a fan of mildly spicy red wines like Shiraz, meet your brand new squeeze. It's all about berries, and concentration of fruit. It's clean, it's round, it's voluptuous, it's about all those big things without being too heavy.

John Torode
Beef rendang with lemongrass and ginger, Thai herb salad and sticky rice

This is an impressive yet simple dish. The sticky rice is a revelation.

Ingredients Serves 4

Beef rendang
1 lemongrass stalk, chopped
20g (¾ oz) coriander seeds
½ teaspoon cumin seeds
½ teaspoon turmeric powder
50g (2oz) block coconut cream
1½ large onions, sliced
3 garlic cloves, chopped
3 red chillies, chopped
1 thumb-sized piece of fresh root ginger, peeled and chopped
1 bay leaf
750g (1Ib 10oz) beef shin, boneless and cut into 2.5cm (1 inch) cubes
400g (14oz) coconut milk
250ml (9fl oz) hot beef stock

Sticky rice
200g (7oz) Thai jasmine rice
200g (7oz) sticky rice
1 teaspoon salt

Salad
110g (4oz) Chinese cabbage
2 deseeded chillies and 2 lime leaves cut into julienne strips
25g (1oz) pea shoots
50g (2oz) mizuna leaves
Small handful each of fresh mint, coriander and Thai basil leaves
1 spring onion, sliced
50g (2oz) green beans, cut into 2cm (¾ inch) pieces
Small handful of beansprouts

Dressing
Juice of 1 lime
1 teaspoon sunflower oil
1 teaspoon Thai fish sauce
1 red chilli, deseeded and finely chopped
1 garlic clove, finely sliced

Method

Beef rendang
Pound the lemongrass to a pulp using a mortar and pestle / Gently toast the coriander and cumin seeds and the turmeric in a dry frying pan until fragrant, then grind to a powder or pound with a pestle until the spices are as smooth as possible / In a wide pan (such as a cast-iron wok), heat the block of coconut cream until it melts, keeping the heat low so it does not burn / Drop in the onions, garlic, chillies, ginger and pounded lemongrass and cook gently until the onions have softened and the mixture starts to release its aroma / Add the ground spices and the bay leaf and cook for a few minutes more / Add the meat, increase the heat so it browns well, and stir until completely coated with the spices – this will take a few minutes / Add the coconut milk, bring to the boil, then add the hot stock / Turn the heat up to high and continue cooking – the level of the liquid will quickly fall / Stir occasionally until the sauce is reduced to a thick paste, then keep cooking and stirring until the sauce becomes thick and really coats the meat – at least 1–1½ hours.

Sticky rice
Half an hour before you want to serve the beef, wash the rice 3 times and drain / Place the rice in a saucepan and cover with 800ml (1½ pints) water / Add the salt and cover with a lid / Place on the heat and bring to the boil / Boil for 5 minutes, without lifting the lid, then turn the heat off and steam for 20 minutes.

Salad and dressing
While the rice is steaming, shred the cabbage then toss all the salad ingredients together in a bowl / Mix all the dressing ingredients together in a bowl.

To serve

Toss the salad in the dressing / Pile the sticky rice on to serving plates and spoon the beef rendang alongside / Serve the salad separately.

Wine expert Olly Smith's choice
Viñalba Malbec Reserva
Matching a red meat with a white wine sounds a bit kinky but don't worry about the sweetness, the red chillies will strip that away and make this a crisp, refreshing accompaniment to this spicy dish.

James Martin
Chilli beef with spicy noodles

This dish was one of James's biggest hits with the *Saturday Kitchen* crew. Try it yourself and you'll never order another takeaway version again!

Ingredients Serves 4

Chilli beef
400g (14oz) beef fillet, cut into thin strips
2 tablespoons vegetable oil
4 tablespoons Sichuan peppercorns
Zest of 2 oranges
1 teaspoon salt
8 tablespoons rice flour, potato flour or cornflour
2 carrots, cut into fine julienne strips

Sauce
150ml (5fl oz) rice wine vinegar
150g (5oz) caster sugar
4 tablespoons soy sauce
2 red chillies, deseeded and finely diced
2 teaspoons chilli flakes
10cm (4 inch) piece of fresh root ginger, finely grated

Noodles
1 tablespoon vegetable oil
10cm (4 inch) piece of fresh root ginger, finely shredded
4 garlic cloves, finely chopped
6 spring onions, finely sliced
250g (9oz) fine egg noodles, cooked according to packet instructions, then drained and refreshed
3 tablespoons sesame oil
2 tablespoons soy sauce
2 tablespoons rice wine vinegar
Juice of ½ lemon
2 tablespoons sesame seeds
4 tablespoons roughly chopped fresh coriander

Method

Chilli beef
Heat a deep-fat fryer to 190°C / Toss the beef strips in the vegetable oil / Heat a frying pan until hot, add the Sichuan peppercorns and toast for 1 minute / Place in a pestle and mortar and crush thoroughly, then add the orange zest and crush once more / Place the salt and flour in a bowl, add the Sichuan mixture and mix well to combine / Add the beef and toss to coat each piece thoroughly / Drop the beef into the deep-fat fryer a few batches at a time, and cook for 2 minutes / Drain on kitchen paper / Drop the carrot julienne into the fryer and cook for 1–2 minutes, until just softened and floating back to the surface of the oil / Drain on kitchen paper and set aside.

Sauce
Heat a frying pan, add the vinegar, sugar and soy sauce and bring to the boil / Add the chillies, chilli flakes and ginger and cook for a few minutes until just thickened / Add the cooked beef and carrots to the sauce and cook for 1–2 minutes, tossing to coat everything.

Noodles
While you make the sauce, heat a wok until hot, add the vegetable oil, ginger, garlic and spring onions and stir-fry for 2 minutes until softened / Add the noodles and stir-fry for 1 minute / Add the sesame oil, soy sauce, rice wine vinegar and lemon juice and toss well / Add the sesame seeds and cook for another 1–2 minutes until hot / Add the coriander and mix well.

To serve

Pile the noodles on to serving plates and spoon the beef alongside, spooning extra sauce over the top.

Wine expert Susy Atkins's choice
Chileno Merlot Rose

James Martin
Thai red penang curry

Everyone should have a Thai curry in their recipe repertoire; this is a fusion of Thai and Malay flavours that makes the perfect red curry.

Ingredients Serves 4

Paste
1 large shallot, roughly chopped
3cm (1¼ inch) piece of galangal, peeled and roughly chopped
2 bird's-eye chillies, deseeded and roughly chopped
3 garlic cloves
2 kaffir lime leaves, roughly chopped
1 tablespoon soy sauce
2 tablespoons fish sauce
1 teaspoon shrimp paste
4 tablespoons tomato purée
1 tablespoon paprika
1 tablespoon ground cumin
1 tablespoon ground coriander
½ teaspoon ground cinnamon
½ teaspoon turmeric
¼ teaspoon ground nutmeg
¼ teaspoon ground cloves

Beef
1 tablespoon groundnut oil
500g (1lb 2oz) beef fillet, thinly sliced
400ml (14fl oz) coconut milk
1–2 tablespoons Thai fish sauce
Juice of 1 lime
Small handful of Thai basil leaves, roughly torn

To serve
300g (11oz) Thai jasmine rice, cooked according to the packet instructions

Method

Paste
Place all the ingredients in a food processor or pestle and mortar and blitz to a smooth purée.

Beef
Heat a wok, add the oil and beef and stir-fry until just browned / Add the paste and cook for 1–2 minutes / Add the coconut milk, bring to the boil and simmer for 2–3 minutes / Add the fish sauce and lime juice to taste / Ladle the curry into a bowl and top with the Thai basil leaves.

To serve
Ladle on to plates, with the Thai jasmine rice alongside.

Nick Nairn
Beef fillet with coconut milk served with baby gems, crispy noodles and dipping sauce

This is a great dish for supper any time, but would work well for entertaining.

Ingredients Serves 4

Beef
200g (7oz) beef fillet, thinly
    sliced
1 tablespoon olive oil
75ml (3fl oz) coconut milk

Dipping sauce
2.5cm (1 inch) piece of fresh
    root ginger
50g (2oz) cashew nuts
110ml (4fl oz) rice wine
    vinegar
110g (4oz) caster sugar
50ml (2fl oz) Thai fish sauce
2 teaspoons chilli flakes
1 small bunch of fresh
    coriander, roughly chopped

Noodles
40g (1½oz) dried rice noodles

To serve

2 baby gem lettuces

Method

Beef
Toss the beef in some salt and pepper and the olive oil / Heat a frying pan and seal the beef – avoid fiddling with it too much as you want to allow it to develop a nice crust, and move it too soon and it'll stick to the pan / Once the beef is browned, add the coconut milk, then reduce the heat and cook for 4–5 minutes, stirring occasionally – the coconut milk will reduce down to give a sticky consistency, coating the beef.

Dipping sauce
Grate the ginger, unpeeled, into the middle of a piece of muslin / Fold over the muslin to create a piping bag shape, hold over a bowl, and squeeze out the juice from the ginger into a small bowl by slowly twisting the muslin with the ginger inside / Next, crush the nuts in a pestle and mortar – some chunky bits are good for crunch, so don't process them too much / Put the rice wine vinegar into a pan with the caster sugar, and stir / Add the fish sauce, chilli flakes and ginger juice and cook on a low heat for 5 minutes / Add the chopped nuts and heat for a further minute / Finally throw in the chopped coriander and heat for a final minute.

Noodles
Heat oil in a deep-fat fryer to 180°C (if you don't have a thermometer, drop in a single noodle and it should puff up in 2–3 seconds, without burning) / Add the noodles to the oil (they will expand quickly and dramatically) / Lift the noodles out using a strainer and transfer to a baking sheet lined with kitchen paper to drain.

To serve

Divide up the leaves from the baby gems and lay out on your serving plates / Spoon the beef on to the baby gem leaves, and drizzle the dipping sauce over / Scrunch the crispy noodles over the plates and serve.

Wine expert Tim Atkin's choice
Leasingham Magnus Riesling
I'm going for a dry, aromatic white wine with absolutely no oak. There's a lot of character in this one, but not so much that it's going to clash with the Thai flavours.

James Martin
Braised oxtail and beetroot with creamy mash

Cuts like oxtail take longer to cook but they are well worth the investment of time, as you'll be rewarded with a deep rich flavour.

Ingredients Serves 4

Oxtail

50g (2oz) butter
2 onions, diced
2 garlic cloves, roughly chopped
2 large carrots, cut into chunks
350g (12oz) raw beetroot, peeled and cut into wedges
2 bay leaves
2 sprigs of thyme
2 tablespoons tomato purée
1.5kg (3Ib 4oz) oxtail, cut into pieces
3 tablespoons plain flour
1½ teaspoons mustard powder
500ml (18fl oz) red wine
3 tablespoons Worcestershire sauce
5 drops of Tabasco
450ml (16fl oz) beef stock

Mash

1 kg (2lb 2oz) King Edward potatoes, peeled and cut into chunks
75g (3oz) butter
150ml (5fl oz) milk

To serve

50–75g (2–3oz) butter

Method

Oxtail

Preheat the oven to 170°C/325°F/Gas 3 / Heat a large ovenproof casserole dish, add half the butter and the onions and sweat until just softened / Add the garlic, carrots, beetroot, bay leaves, thyme and tomato purée, and cook for 2–3 minutes / Toss the oxtail with the flour, mustard powder and some salt and black pepper / Heat a frying pan, add the remaining butter and the oxtail in batches and fry until browned / Remove each batch from the pan and add to the vegetables, along with any remaining seasoned flour / Deglaze the frying pan with the red wine, scraping the bottom to remove any residue / Pour on to the vegetables and stir well, then add the Worcestershire sauce, Tabasco and beef stock / Bring to the boil, then cover and place in the oven for 3 hours – or longer if possible / Season with salt and black pepper.

Mash

Place the potatoes in a large saucepan and cover with water / Add a pinch of salt, place on the heat and bring to the boil / Simmer for 15 minutes, until tender / Drain and return to the pan over the heat to drive off any excess moisture / Mash well, adding the butter and milk, and season with salt and black pepper.

To serve

Pile the mash on to soup plates and top with a knob of butter / Spoon the oxtail next to the mash with plenty of the juices and vegetables.

Wine expert Peter Richards's choice
Otra Vida Malbec

Gennaro Contaldo
La gran lasagna

This dish is one of Gennaro's family favourites, and it'll be a hit at home for you too.

Ingredients Serves 6–8

Tomato sauce
125ml (4½fl oz) olive oil
2 medium onions, finely chopped
4 x 400g (14oz) tins of plum tomatoes
1 large bunch of fresh basil leaves, roughly torn

Meatballs
250g (9oz) minced beef
250g (9oz) minced pork
4 garlic cloves, finely chopped
3 tablespoons roughly chopped fresh parsley
1 egg, beaten
Olive oil, for frying
Flour, for dusting

Lasagne
500g (1lb 2oz) fresh lasagne sheets
200g (7oz) Parmesan, grated
4 hard-boiled eggs, sliced
200g (7oz) ricotta
4 mozzarella balls, roughly chopped

Method

Tomato sauce
Heat the olive oil in a large pan, add the onions and sweat until softened / Add the tomatoes and basil, season with salt and pepper, then reduce the heat and simmer gently for about 25 minutes / Set aside.

Meatballs
While the sauce is simmering, place the beef, pork, garlic, parsley and egg in a bowl and mix well together / Shape into small balls about the size of walnuts / Heat some olive oil in a large frying pan / Dust the meatballs with flour and fry in the hot oil until golden all over – do this in batches, a few at a time, depending on the size of your frying pan / Drain on kitchen paper and set aside.

Lasagne
Preheat the oven to 200°C/400°F/Gas 6 / Spread some of the tomato sauce in the base of a large ovenproof dish / Place a layer of pasta sheets on top of the sauce, then spoon more sauce over / Sprinkle with Parmesan, and arrange a few egg slices, a few meatballs, a few knobs of ricotta and some pieces of mozzarella on top / Cover with more pasta sheets and repeat the layers with the remaining ingredients, finishing with tomato sauce, meatballs, eggs and cheese / Cover with foil and bake in the oven for about 30 minutes / Remove the foil and cook for a further 5 minutes, until the cheese has melted nicely over the top / Serve immediately.

Wine expert Peter Richards's choice
Mas Las Cabes Côtes du Roussillon
With this wine there are loads of lovely ripe fruit aromas, but there's also a juiciness and a freshness to match the acidity of the tomatoes. It works equally well as an everyday drink or a special occasion wine.

James Martin
Bourbon glazed sticky ribs with coleslaw and baked potato

This is heavenly, best enjoyed with close friends as it's pretty messy! If you can't get hold of chipotle chilli ketchup, any chilli ketchup will do.

Ingredients Serves 4

Ribs
1.5kg (3lb 4oz) beef foreribs
1 teaspoon black peppercorns
3 bay leaves
1 small bunch of fresh flat-leaf parsley
1 onion, roughly chopped
1 carrot, cut into chunks
175g (6oz) tomato ketchup
150g (5oz) chipotle chilli ketchup
110ml (4fl oz) dark soy sauce
175g (6oz) honey
4 tablespoons teriyaki sauce
4 tablespoons bourbon

Potatoes
4 large baking potatoes
1 tablespoon olive oil
1 teaspoon salt

Coleslaw
2 egg yolks
1 tablespoon white wine vinegar
1 tablespoon Dijon mustard
200ml (7fl oz) rapeseed oil
90ml (3½fl oz) olive oil
2 tablespoons cold water
Juice of ½ lemon
250g (9oz) carrot, finely shredded
300g (11oz) white cabbage, finely shredded
1 sweet white onion, finely sliced

To serve
250ml (9fl oz) soured cream
4 tablespoons finely chopped fresh curly parsley

Method

Ribs
Place the ribs in a large saucepan with the peppercorns, bay leaves, parsley, onion and carrot / Cover with water and place on the heat / Bring to the boil, then reduce the heat and simmer for 1½ hours / Meanwhile, preheat the oven to 200°C/400°F/Gas 6 / Place the ketchups, soy sauce, honey, teriyaki and bourbon in a saucepan and bring to a simmer / Take the ribs from the saucepan, dip into the sauce to coat, and place in a roasting tin / Place in the oven for 20 minutes, basting with more sauce halfway through.

Potatoes
When the ribs are halfway through their simmering time, pierce the potatoes in a couple of places, then rub with the olive oil and salt / Place on the top shelf in the oven for 1 hour / To check if tender, pierce with a knife – if there is still some resistance, return to the oven for a further 10 minutes, then repeat.

Coleslaw
While the ribs and potatoes are cooking, blend the egg yolks, vinegar and mustard in a food processor with a pinch of salt / With the processor running, slowly pour in the oils until the texture changes to a thick mayonnaise / Whisk in the water and lemon juice and check the seasoning / Place the carrots, cabbage and onion in a bowl and add enough mayonnaise to coat / Season with salt and black pepper.

To serve

Pile the ribs on to serving plates, along with a spoonful of coleslaw / Split the potatoes in half, top with a dollop of soured cream and a little chopped parsley, and serve alongside the ribs.

Wine expert Susy Atkins's choice
Ravenswood Lodi Zinfandel

Fernando Stovell
Aztec's molcajete

Most incarnations of Mexican food known in Britain are actually Tex-Mex. Fernando cooks real Mexican, and it doesn't get more authentic than this dish.

Ingredients Serves 4

Salsa
2 large garlic cloves
1 chipotle chilli
½ Spanish onion, roughly chopped
1 bunch of fresh coriander
1 tomato, peeled, quartered and deseeded
50ml (2fl oz) Corona beer
300g (11oz) tinned peeled tomatoes

Refried beans
4 tablespoons sunflower oil
½ onion, roughly chopped
2 x 400g (14oz) tins of red kidney beans in water (discard the water from 1 of the tins)
75ml (3fl oz) chicken stock

Meat
1 chicken breast, cut into strips
1 tablespoon olive oil
200g (7oz) sirloin steak
150g (5oz) spicy chorizo, sliced lengthways
1 bunch of spring onions

To serve
8 tortillas
1 large avocado, peeled, pitted and sliced lengthways
1 small bunch of fresh coriander
1 lime

Method

Salsa
Place the garlic, chipotle chilli, onion and coriander in a pestle and mortar and crush to a paste / Add the fresh tomato and crush together, then add the beer and tinned tomatoes and season with salt and black pepper / Transfer this mixture to a saucepan (or a lava stone pestle), place on the heat and bring to the boil / Reduce the heat and simmer for 20 minutes / Check the seasoning.

Refried beans
While the salsa is simmering, heat a saucepan, add the sunflower oil and onion and cook until golden brown / Add the beans, along with the water from 1 of the tins / Stir, add the chicken stock and bring to the boil, then reduce the heat and simmer for 5–8 minutes / Purée in a blender or food processor, season with salt and black pepper, and set aside.

Meat
Heat a griddle pan, then toss the chicken strips with olive oil and some salt and pepper, and add to the pan / Season the steak with salt and black pepper, then add the steak and chorizo to the griddle pan / Cook for 2–3 minutes, then turn the meat over and cook for a further 2–3 minutes / Remove from the griddle pan and set aside / Add the spring onions and griddle for 1–2 minutes.

To serve

Toast the tortillas over a naked flame or under the grill / The salsa should either be served hot in the lava stone pestle, or if you've been using a saucepan, pour it into a normal pestle and mortar or a large warmed bowl to serve / Slice the steak and add to the salsa in the pestle along with the chorizo and chicken / Garnish the top with the grilled spring onions, avocado and coriander / Place the warmed refried beans in a separate bowl and serve with the toasted tortillas and a wedge of lime.

Wine expert Olly Smith's choice
L.A. Cetto Petite Sirah
Petite Sirah is also known as Duriff. It has dark flavours and a robust texture but with a little edge of finesse. The chunky structure will work brilliantly with the sirloin steak and the mellowness won't swamp the chicken.

John Campbell
Slow-cooked beef with horseradish mash, mushroom tortellini, buttered cabbage and red wine sauce

John's demonstration of cooking with clingfilm really impressed the *Saturday Kitchen* crew, which says a lot, as we've seen some amazing displays of skill on the show.

Ingredients Serves 4

Beef
1 tablespoon corn oil
500g (1lb 2oz) middle cut well-hung beef

Horseradish mash
500g (1lb 2oz) potatoes, peeled and cut into 5cm (2 inch) dice
200ml (7fl oz) double cream
½–1 horseradish root, grated, to taste

Wild mushroom filling
175g (6oz) boneless skinless chicken breast, diced
125ml (4½fl oz) whipping cream
110g (4oz) wild mushrooms, sautéd for 2 minutes in a little olive oil
1 teaspoon chopped fresh flat-leaf parsley

Pasta
550g (1lb 4oz) 'OO' pasta flour
5 egg yolks
4 whole eggs

Red wine sauce
110g (4oz) butter
250g (9oz) shallots, sliced
250g (9oz) button mushrooms
500ml (18fl oz) red wine, reduced to 200ml (7fl oz)
500ml (18fl oz) good-quality beef stock

Method

Beef
Preheat the oven to 55–60°C / Heat a frying pan, add the corn oil and brown the beef on all sides – no more than 2 minutes in total / Remove from the pan and allow to cool / Wrap the fillet in clingfilm and place in a roasting tin in the oven for 50–60 minutes (this process will achieve a medium-rare fillet with a core temperature of 57–59°C) / Test the meat with a digital meat thermometer – if the 57–59°C temperature has not been reached, increase the heat in the oven slightly and return the beef to the oven for a further 10 minutes, before checking once more / Repeat until the temperature has been reached / Remove from the oven, remove the clingfilm and re-seal the fillet in a hot frying pan – this should take no more than 30 seconds.

Horseradish mash
When you have put the beef into the oven, put the potatoes into a pan of cold water, bring to the boil, then drain and wash in cold water / Place the washed potatoes in cold water again and bring to about 80°C (you should see steam coming up off the pan but there is no movement in the water) / Cook for 1½ hours, then drain, return to the pan to dry slightly, then remove from the heat / Pass the potatoes through a ricer or mash them, and add the cream and horseradish to taste / Season with salt and black pepper and spoon into a piping bag.

Wild mushroom filling
While the beef is cooking, place the chicken breast in a food processor and process for 20 seconds, until it is loosely minced / Add the cream and a little salt and continue to process – no more than 30 seconds / Turn the machine to the pulse setting and add the cooked wild mushrooms and chopped parsley / Take a little of the filling, wrap it in clingfilm and poach in a little water for 2 minutes to check if the seasoning is correct / Place the rest of the filling in the fridge until you are ready to use it.

Pasta
Once the filling is made, place the pasta flour in a bowl and make a well in the middle / In a separate bowl, beat together the egg yolks and whole eggs / Pour the egg mix into the well and fold in the flour to form a ball, then knead for about 5 minutes / Allow to rest for as long as possible – you can cut the pasta into portions and freeze any extra / When ready to use, roll out a pasta portion to no. 1 on the machine and cut it into discs / Place a disc of pasta on a board, brush the edge with water and place a teaspoon of filling in the centre / Top with another pasta disc, press down around the edges and fold the edges over / Repeat with the remaining pasta and filling / When the beef and potatoes are ready, bring a pan of salted water to the boil, add the tortellini and simmer for 3 minutes / Remove from the pan and drain on kitchen paper.

Ingredients (continued)

Cabbage
½ Savoy cabbage
40g (1½oz) butter
1 carrot, finely diced
1 shallot, finely sliced
1 bay leaf
1 sprig of fresh thyme
250ml (9fl oz) chicken stock

To serve

Parsley cress (or very small-
    leaved watercress)

Method (continued)

Red wine sauce
Once your tortellini are made and waiting to be cooked, heat a frying pan, add the butter, shallots and mushrooms and fry until golden / Drain in a colander to get rid of the fat then return to the pan / Add the red wine and beef stock, bring to the boil and cook for 10 minutes / Pass through a sieve, return to the pan, season with salt and black pepper and keep warm.

Cabbage
When you are nearly ready to serve the beef, blanch the cabbage in boiling water for 3 minutes / Melt the butter in another pan, add the carrot and shallot and cook for 2 minutes, then add the blanched cabbage, bay leaf, thyme and chicken stock / Bring to the boil, and cook until the liquor is reduced and the cabbage is cooked – roughly 5 minutes / Season with salt and pepper.

To serve

Drain any excess liquid away from the cabbage and place a portion in the centre of each serving bowl / Pipe a mound of mashed potato next to it / Carve the beef and place next to the cabbage and mash / Arrange the tortellini next to the mash, on top of the cabbage / Finish the dish with the red wine sauce and parsley cress.

Wine expert Olly Smith's choice
Viñalba Malbec Reserva
This wine mimics the texture of beef fillet. It's dense and it's juicy and it doesn't have a whole stack of tannin to get in there and rummage with the beef. This is perfectly balanced for the job.

Michael Caines
Pan-fried veal fillet with wild mushrooms, asparagus, wild garlic and a sherry sauce

A perfect example of Michelin-starred food that you can create at home. This will become a classic in your repertoire.

Ingredients Serves 4

Sherry sauce
110g (4oz) butter
75g (3oz) shallots, sliced
10 sprigs of fresh thyme
110g (4oz) button mushrooms, sliced
200ml (7fl oz) dry Amontillado sherry
200ml (7fl oz) chicken stock
200ml (7fl oz) cream

Veal and asparagus
4 x 175g (6oz) rose veal fillets, cut into medallions
110g (4oz) butter
1 tablespoon olive oil
20 garlic cloves, peeled and blanched 3 times (cold water up to the boil, then refresh in cold water and repeat)
1 sprig of fresh thyme
20 asparagus tips, peeled and trimmed
150g (5oz) mixed wild mushrooms – mousserons, girolles, pied bleu, etc.
110g (4oz) wild garlic
110g (4oz) baby leaf spinach

Method

Sherry sauce
Heat a frying pan, add half the butter and all the shallots, and cook until soft and transparent / Add the thyme sprigs and mushrooms and cook until the mushrooms are slippery in texture / Add the sherry and cook until the liquid is reduced by half / Add the chicken stock and reduce by half again / Add the cream and again reduce by half, then whisk in the remaining butter / Pass through a fine sieve into a saucepan and season with salt and pepper, then set aside.

Veal and asparagus
Season the veal medallions with salt and black pepper / Heat a frying pan and add a third of the butter, the oil and the veal / Cook for 2–3 minutes on each side, until golden brown / Add the garlic and thyme towards the end and cook until golden and tender / Remove the meat and garlic and set aside / Spoon off any excess fat from the pan, and deglaze with 3 tablespoons of water / Add this to the sherry sauce and reheat, whisking all the time / Meanwhile, bring a shallow pan of water to the boil and add another third of the butter and the asparagus / Cook gently for 2–3 minutes, until just tender, then drain / Heat a separate frying pan until hot, add the last of the butter, the mushrooms, wild garlic and spinach and sauté for 2–3 minutes, until the mushrooms are cooked and the leaves have wilted / Season with salt and black pepper.

To serve

Spoon some of the mushroom mixture into the centre of each serving plate and top with the veal medallions / Spoon a little more of the mushroom mixture on top and place the asparagus to one side / Scatter with the cooked garlic and finally spoon over the sauce.

Wine expert Peter Richards's choice
Baron de Ley Rioja Reserva
The veal really needs a red wine and it's got to be Rioja. This wine is quite mature and it has mushroomy, gamey, sort of earthy characteristics, which are exactly what we're looking for – delicious.

James Martin
Veal chops with spätzle

Spätzle (small dumplings) are quite quick and straightforward to make, but your friends and family will be impressed you made the effort.

Ingredients Serves 4

Sauce

300ml (11fl oz) beef or veal stock
110ml (4fl oz) red wine
50g (2oz) butter

Veal

4 veal chops, trimmed
2 tablespoons olive oil
2 tablespoons roughly chopped fresh dill
2 tablespoons roughly chopped fresh chervil
2 tablespoons roughly chopped fresh chives
75g (3oz) Japanese breadcrumbs
50g (2oz) butter

Spätzle

500g (1lb 2oz) plain flour
4 eggs
2 tablespoons double cream
2 tablespoons chopped fresh dill
2 tablespoons chopped fresh chives
2 tablespoons chopped fresh chervil
50g (2oz) butter
2 tablespoons olive oil

Method

Sauce

Place the stock in a saucepan, bring to the boil and simmer until reduced by two-thirds / Add the red wine and repeat, cooking until reduced by two-thirds again / Whisk in the butter, season with salt and black pepper and keep warm.

Veal

Preheat the oven to 200°C/400°F/Gas 6 / Season the veal chops with salt and black pepper, then massage in the olive oil / Toss the herbs and breadcrumbs together and press on to the chops / Heat an ovenproof frying pan, add the butter and the chops and fry on each side until golden / Transfer to a roasting tray and place in the oven for 8–10 minutes.

Spätzle

While the veal is cooking, place all the spätzle ingredients in a food processor and blitz to a dough / Season with salt and black pepper / Bring a saucepan of salted water to the boil / Place a spoonful of the dough on a board, then, using a palette knife, form the dough into little rolls / Drop directly into the boiling water and boil for 1–1½ minutes / Drain and refresh in iced water / Heat a frying pan until hot, add the butter, olive oil and spätzle and fry for 1–2 minutes.

To serve

Place a veal chop on each serving plate / Arrange the spätzle alongside and finish with a spoonful of red wine sauce.

Stuart Gillies
Griddled veal rump with roasted ceps and mixed leaf and walnut salad

Ceps are one of the finest eating mushroom varieties and so can be quite pricey, but they're worth every penny in this delicious dish.

Ingredients Serves 4

Veal and ceps
4 x 200g (7oz) veal rump steaks
3 tablespoons olive oil
1 sprig of fresh rosemary, leaves picked
150g (5oz) fresh ceps, cleaned and thickly sliced
3 garlic cloves, crushed
75g (3oz) butter
25g (1oz) fresh flat-leaf parsley, roughly chopped
Juice of 1 lemon

Salad
1 head of chicory 'Castelfranco', leaves picked and torn
1 batavia lettuce, leaves picked and torn
1 head of Trevisano or radicchio, leaves picked and torn
75g (3oz) walnut halves, lightly crushed
1 tablespoon sherry vinegar
2 tablespoons olive oil
2 tablespoons walnut oil

Method

Veal and ceps
Heat a griddle pan / Coat the veal with half the olive oil and the rosemary leaves / Season well with salt and black pepper and place directly on the griddle / Cook for 1–2 minutes on each side, then remove to a plate and set aside / Meanwhile, heat a frying pan and add the remaining olive oil and the ceps / Cook for 2–3 minutes, until browned, then season with a little salt and black pepper / Add the crushed garlic and butter, reduce the heat and cook for 1 minute / Add the chopped parsley and lemon juice and stir to combine, then check the seasoning.

Salad
Toss the salad leaves with the walnuts in a bowl / Whisk the vinegar, olive oil and walnut oil together in a small bowl and drizzle over the leaves.

To serve

Cut the veal into slices on the diagonal and place on serving plates / Spoon the ceps over the top and finish with a pile of salad.

Wine expert Susie Barrie's choice
Tesco Finest Barbera D'Asti Superiore
This is a wine with fresh acidity but it's also got a backbone of tannin and plenty of ripe fruit to complement the meaty veal. There's just a subtle earthy flavour, which will be perfect with the garlicky ceps and the walnuts.

Arthur Potts Dawson
Beaten loin of pork with artichoke and courgettes braised with thyme and lemon zest

Tana Ramsay
Red pepper and apple meatballs with sweet and sour sauce

Ken Hom
Pineapple pork with noodles

Bill Granger
Pork meatballs with curry sauce

James Martin
Pan-fried pork fillet with prune and Armagnac sauce and sautéd potatoes

Galton Blackiston
Fillet of Blythburgh pork with honey and sesame seeds, carrot and ginger sauce and crispy potatoes

Atul Kochhar
Tandoori spice marinated grilled pork chops with Savoy cabbage poriyal and apple-porcini salad

Rachel Allen
Pork and mushroom pie with gentle spices and Gujarati style French beans

Si King
Fruit gammon with a spiced marmalade glaze and two zingy salsas

Glynn Purnell
Roast loin of pork fillet with carrots cooked in toffee, cumin and passion fruit with smoked salt and borage leaves

Matt Tebbutt
Old Spot pork cooked with milk, cinnamon, bay and lemon

Martin Blunos
Boiled collar of bacon with veggies and dumplings

James Martin
Spiced pot-roasted pork loin with sautéd potatoes and roasted carrots

Pork

Arthur Potts Dawson
Beaten loin of pork with artichoke and courgettes braised with thyme and lemon zest

Eco-friendly chef Arthur recycles food scraps in on-site wormeries at his restaurants. This dish is so delicious though, we doubt there'll be leftovers when you make it.

Ingredients Serves 4

Artichokes and courgettes
12 small violet artichokes
Extra virgin olive oil
12 small courgettes
4 garlic cloves
Zest of 1 lemon
1 small bunch of fresh thyme, chopped
4 small dried chillies, crumbled

Pork
4 x 175g (6oz) pork loin
Zest of 1 lemon
1 small bunch of fresh thyme, leaves picked and chopped

To serve
1 punnet of micro cress
Extra virgin olive oil, to drizzle

Method

Artichokes and courgettes
Peel away all the outer leaves of the artichokes to reveal the heart / With a small sharp knife, trim the outside of the heart to reveal the tender, pale green flesh / Cut the top off the heart to reveal the choke (the furry leaves inside the centre) / Use a teaspoon to scoop out the choke and discard / Trim the stem to 2cm in length and remove the tough outer layer with a knife / Cut the prepared artichokes in half lengthways then cut each half in 2 lengthways to create 4 wedges / Heat a little olive oil in a frying pan and gently fry the artichokes for 2–3 minutes / Wash the courgettes, cut to the same size as the artichokes and add to the pan as the artichokes are just starting to be cooked / Add the garlic, lemon zest, chopped thyme, chillies, a splash of water and some more olive oil, then season to taste and keep warm.

Pork
Trim the pork loins and slice each into 4 pieces, then lay them between 2 pieces of clingfilm and beat until paper thin / Lay the pieces on a plate and season with lemon zest, chopped thyme, salt and black pepper / Heat a griddle pan and quickly sear the pork on both sides.

To serve

Arrange the artichokes and courgettes on serving plates, alternating with the slices of pork / Snip some micro cress on to the plate and finish with a drizzle of olive oil.

Wine expert Susie Barrie's choice
Reuilly, Henri Beurdin
This has got plenty of lemony acidity to cope with the difficult, intense flavours of the artichokes – and there are lots of grassy, herbal flavours that are ideal with the thyme, courgette and garlic.

Tana Ramsay
Red pepper and apple meatballs with sweet and sour sauce

Great for all the family, including your Michelin-starred husband, if you have one!

Ingredients Serves 4

Meatballs

450g (1lb) lean lamb mince
450g (1lb) lean pork mince
1 red pepper, deseeded and finely chopped
1 small onion, finely chopped
3 Cox's apples, peeled and finely grated
1 tablespoon grated fresh root ginger
4 teaspoons chopped fresh coriander
1 egg white
3 tablespoons flour
1 tablespoon olive oil

Sauce

2 teaspoons olive oil
1 red onion, finely chopped
4 baby leeks, chopped
1 courgette, sliced
450g (1lb) cherry tomatoes, halved
2 teaspoons brown sugar
2 teaspoons malt vinegar

To serve

Basmati rice, cooked
6 basil leaves, torn

Method

Meatballs

Place the lamb and pork mince in a bowl and mix together / Add the red pepper, onion, apples, ginger, coriander and egg white and mix well / Shape into small balls, about 2cm (1 inch) in diameter / Place on a plate and dust with the flour, rolling to cover all sides / Put into the fridge for 30 minutes to firm up / Heat a frying pan, add the olive oil and meatballs and fry until golden brown all over, about 5 or 6 minutes.

Sauce

While the meatballs are firming up in the fridge, heat a frying pan, add the olive oil and red onion and cook for 2 minutes, until just softened / Add the leeks and courgette and fry until coloured slightly / Add the tomatoes, sugar and vinegar, bring to a simmer, and cook for 20 minutes / Place in a liquidiser or food processor and blitz to a purée, then return the purée to the pan / Add the browned meatballs, bring to a simmer, and cook for 15 minutes / While the meatballs are simmering, cook the rice according to the packet instructions.

To serve

Pile the rice on serving plates, top with a ladleful of meatballs and sauce and garnish with a little basil.

Wine expert Peter Richards's choice
Los Molles Carmenere
We're looking for a red here because of all those full meaty flavours. This has lots of lovely ripe and sweet fruit and you might expect it to be a big, bruising monster, but it's really crisp and juicy.

Ken Hom
Pineapple pork with noodles

No one does Chinese food like Ken Hom, and he's always a treat for us on *Saturday Kitchen*. This quick noodle dish is perfect for a week-night supper.

Ingredients Serves 4

Pork

450g (1lb) pork fillet, cut into thin 5cm (2 inch) strips
2 teaspoons light soy sauce
2 teaspoons Shaoxing rice wine or dry sherry
1 teaspoon sesame oil
2 teaspoons cornflour
1½ tablespoons groundnut oil
3 tablespoons coarsely chopped garlic
225g (8oz) fresh or tinned pineapple, chopped
2 tablespoons finely chopped fresh coriander
1 tablespoon dark soy sauce
2 teaspoons sugar

Noodles

250g (9oz) medium egg noodles
2 tablespoons sesame oil
4 spring onions, finely shredded

To serve

Large handful of fresh coriander sprigs

Method

Pork

Place the pork in a bowl, add the light soy sauce, rice wine or sherry, sesame oil and cornflour and toss well, then set aside / Heat a wok or large frying pan over a high heat, add the groundnut oil, and when it is very hot and slightly smoking, add the garlic and stir-fry for 15 seconds or until golden brown / Add the pork and marinade and continue to stir-fry for 3 minutes / Add the pineapple, coriander, dark soy sauce and sugar and continue to stir-fry for 3 minutes more.

Noodles

Meanwhile bring a pan of water to the boil, add the noodles and cook for 2–4 minutes / Drain the noodles and toss with the sesame oil and spring onions.

To serve

Spoon the pork on to serving plates and pile the noodles alongside / Garnish with the coriander sprigs.

Wine expert Peter Richards's choice
Tesco Finest Alsace Pinot Gris
The key flavour in this dish, pineapple, means I need a white wine with tropical fruit flavour. This has lots of lovely honeyed and tropical fruit aromas, and it's got enough freshness to really clean the palate between mouthfuls.

Bill Granger
Pork meatballs with curry sauce

If you're worried the meatballs will fall apart, put them in the fridge for about an hour before cooking so they hold together better.

Ingredients Serves 4–6

Meatballs

600g (1lb 5oz) minced pork
1 onion, grated
1 egg, lightly beaten
50g (2oz) fresh white
   breadcrumbs
1 long red chilli, deseeded and
   finely chopped
2 teaspoons grated fresh root
   ginger
1 teaspoon garam masala
2 tablespoons chopped fresh
   coriander
1 tablespoon grapeseed oil

Curry sauce

3 tablespoons massaman
   curry paste
2 teaspoons grated fresh root
   ginger
4 tomatoes, chopped
200ml (7fl oz) coconut milk
200ml (7fl oz) chicken stock
1 tablespoon lemon juice
2 teaspoons brown sugar

To serve

3–4 tablespoons cashew
   nuts, lightly toasted and
   finely chopped
2 tablespoons chopped fresh
   coriander
Steamed basmati rice

Method

Meatballs

Preheat the oven to 220°C/425°F/Gas 7 / Put all the meatball ingredients except the oil into a large mixing bowl, season with salt and black pepper and mix together well with your hands / Shape into small balls, wetting your hands first to make this easier / Put the meatballs into a large roasting tin, drizzle with the oil and toss gently / Bake in the oven for 15–20 minutes, or until golden.

Curry sauce

While the meatballs are cooking, heat a large frying pan over a medium heat, add the curry paste and ginger and cook, stirring, for 1 minute / Add the tomatoes and cook, stirring occasionally, for a further 2–3 minutes / Add the coconut milk and stock and bring to the boil, then reduce the heat to low and leave to simmer for 5 minutes / When the meatballs are ready, add them to the sauce, stir carefully to make sure they are all coated, and simmer for 20 minutes / Gently stir in the lemon juice and brown sugar.

To serve

Garnish with the cashew nuts and coriander and serve with steamed rice.

Wine expert Susy Atkins's choice
Leitz Riesling Kabinett

This is very fresh, very elegant, rather subtle and sophisticated. It's perfumed with a lifted apple and citrus flavour and very slightly off dry on the finish, which will cut through the richness of this dish.

James Martin
Pan-fried pork fillet with prune and Armagnac sauce and sautéd potatoes

This is a quick, simple dish made special with the addition of sweet prunes and warming Armagnac.

Ingredients Serves 4

Pork
1 jar of prunes in Armagnac
1 pork tenderloin fillet, sliced thinly
25g (1oz) butter
150ml (5fl oz) double cream

Potatoes
25g (1oz) butter
1 tablespoon olive oil
4 potatoes, peeled and cubed
1 shallot, finely chopped
2 tablespoons roughly chopped fresh flat-leaf parsley

Method

Pork
Stone and roughly chop the prunes, reserving 110ml (4fl oz) of the Armagnac / Place the pork slices on a board and flatten, using a meat hammer / Season them with salt and black pepper / Heat a frying pan and add the butter and the pork slices / Fry on each side for 1–2 minutes, until golden and just cooked through / Remove from the pan to a dish and set aside to keep warm / Add the Armagnac to the pan and tip towards the gas flame to ignite the alcohol or, if using an electric or induction oven, place a lit match near the liquid to ignite – either way be careful and stand back from the pan! / Add the prunes and cook for 2 minutes, mashing them down slightly / Add the cream, season with salt and black pepper and cook for a further minute.

Potatoes
Meanwhile heat a separate frying pan until hot and add the butter, olive oil and potatoes / Sauté for 4–5 minutes, until golden brown and tender / Add the shallots and fry for a further minute, then add the parsley / Season with salt and black pepper.

To serve

Place the pork slices on serving plates, spoon over the sauce and pile the potatoes alongside.

Galton Blackiston
Fillet of Blythburgh pork with honey and sesame seeds, carrot and ginger sauce and crispy potatoes

Blythburgh is a free-range, organic breed of pork from Suffolk. You can ask your butcher to order it for you or get it online.

Ingredients Serves 4

Sauce
3 large carrots, peeled and juiced (about 275ml of juice)
5cm (2 inch) piece of fresh root ginger, juiced
25g (1oz) salted butter

Pork
25g (1fl oz) rapeseed oil
25g (1oz) salted butter
2 x 375g (13 oz) pork tenderloin, trimmed
2 tablespoons runny honey
4 tablespoons sesame seeds

Potatoes
50g (2oz) salted butter
2 tablespoons olive oil
4 King Edward potatoes, peeled and cubed
1 sprig of fresh rosemary
1 sprig of fresh thyme
12 garlic cloves, skins left on

Method

Sauce
Put the carrot and ginger juice into a saucepan and simmer to reduce to about 150ml (5fl oz) / Slowly whisk in the butter, then season and set aside.

Pork
Preheat the oven to 200°C/400°F/Gas 6 / Heat a frying pan and add the rapeseed oil and the butter / Once the butter is foaming, add the pork fillets and fry until golden brown on each side / Season with salt and black pepper, then remove from the pan to a plate / Spoon over the honey and coat the pork well with the sesame seeds / Place the pork on a trivet in a roasting tin and cook in the oven for about 9–10 minutes / Remove and set aside to rest for 5 minutes.

Potatoes
While the pork fillets are frying, heat a second frying pan and add the butter, olive oil and potatoes / Fry the potatoes over a high heat so that they start to soften, then add the herb sprigs and garlic and fry until the potatoes are soft and golden.

To serve
Reheat the carrot sauce gently in a small pan / Carve the pork into thick diagonal slices / Spoon some crispy potatoes into the centre of each serving plate / Top with the pork and spoon over the sauce.

Wine expert Susie Barrie's choice
Casillero del Diablo Viognier
What we need is a really good ripe, fruity wine to go with this dish. A wine with soft, spicy, apricot and peach flavours would work really well. This Viognier is perfect, as it is a grape variety that's particularly well known for those flavours.

Ingredients Serves 4

Chops and marinade
1 sprig of fresh thyme
1 tablespoon crushed garlic
1 teaspoon chopped green chillies
1 teaspoon ground fennel seeds
½ teaspoon ground cinnamon
1 sprig of fresh rosemary,
    chopped
3 tablespoons mustard oil
110ml (4fl oz) single cream
50ml (2fl oz) double cream
2 tablespoons gram flour
2 tablespoons Pernod or Ricard
Generous pinch of nutmeg
4 pork chops, fat removed

Cabbage
2 tablespoons oil
1 teaspoon mustard seeds
10 curry leaves
1 teaspoon chopped root ginger
¼ teaspoon turmeric powder
300g (11oz) Savoy cabbage
50g (2oz) freshly grated coconut
1 tablespoon chopped fresh
    coriander leaves
½ tablespoon lemon juice

Salad
2 Granny Smith apples
1 tablespoon lemon juice
½ teaspoon coriander seeds
3 tablespoons olive oil
½ teaspoon chopped garlic
¼ teaspoon dried red chilli flakes
110g (4oz) fresh porcini
    mushrooms
Dash of cider vinegar
Sugar, to taste
½ tablespoon finely chopped
    fresh parsley

To serve
Coriander, Greek, celery and
amaranth cress

Atul Kochhar
Tandoori spice marinated grilled pork chops with Savoy cabbage poriyal and apple-porcini salad

This is Michelin-starred Indian food, the kind of thing you get at Atul's restaurant, Benares. Go on, treat yourself.

Method

Chops and marinade
Preheat the oven to 180°C/350°F/Gas 4 / Remove the thyme leaves from the sprig, then place all the ingredients except the pork chops in a bowl and whisk to combine / Add the chops and toss to coat / Set aside for 30 minutes to marinate / Heat a griddle pan until hot, remove a little of the marinade from the chops so that they are just nicely coated, and add them to the pan / Griddle on each side for 2 minutes, then transfer to an oven tray and place in the oven for 10–15 minutes, until just cooked.

Cabbage
While the chops are in the oven, shred the cabbage, then heat a sauté pan until hot and add the oil, mustard seeds, curry leaves and ginger / Stir until the seeds pop open / Add the turmeric, cabbage and some salt and cook for 10–15 minutes on a low heat until the cabbage has wilted / Remove from the heat and add the coconut, coriander and lemon juice.

Salad
Chop the apples into 2cm (¾ inch) dice and toss them in the lemon juice to prevent them discolouring / Heat a frying pan, toast the coriander seeds and then remove and crush lightly / Add the oil and garlic to the pan and fry until light brown / Add the coriander seeds and chilli / Add the diced apples and sauté for a few minutes to colour lightly, then add the mushrooms / Cook until the mushrooms are browned, then add the cider vinegar and season with salt and sugar / Remove from the heat, add the chopped parsley, transfer to a bowl and set aside.

To serve

Place some cabbage in the centre of each serving plate / Arrange the pork chops on top of the cabbage / Place some of the apple and porcini salad alongside, and spoon over the liquid from the bowl / Sprinkle the mixed cress on top of the salad and serve immediately.

Wine expert Susie Barrie's choice
Yalumba Y Series Viognier
This is packed with apricot, white peach and lime blossom flavours, and there's just a hint of ginger, which is quite typical of this grape variety. It will be great with the delicate curry.

Rachel Allen
Pork and mushroom pie with gentle spices and Gujarati style French beans

This is a really tasty pie and the beans would make an interesting accompaniment to a range of dishes.

Ingredients Serves 4

Filling
135g (4¾oz) butter
110g (4oz) plain flour
2 onions, chopped
1 teaspoon ground cumin
1 teaspoon ground coriander
700g (1½lb) pork (shoulder or leg), fat removed, cut into 1–2cm (½–¾ inch) cubes
250ml (9fl oz) chicken stock
1 tablespoon olive oil
300g (11oz) button mushrooms, sliced (leave them whole or halve them if they are small)
250ml (9fl oz) single cream
1 tablespoon chopped fresh parsley

Mash
1kg (2lb 2oz) floury potatoes
50g (2oz) butter
200ml (7fl oz) boiling milk, or 150ml (¼ pint) boiling milk and 50ml (2fl oz) single cream

Beans
1lb (450g) green beans, cut into 2.5cm (1 inch) pieces
4 tablespoons vegetable oil
1 tablespoon whole black mustard seeds
4 garlic cloves, peeled and very finely chopped
1 hot dried red chilli, coarsely crushed in a mortar
1 teaspoon salt
1 teaspoon sugar

Method

Filling
Heat a saucepan over a medium heat and melt 110g (4 oz) of the butter then add the flour, stirring continuously / Allow to cook for 2 minutes then pour the roux into a bowl / Preheat the oven to 170°C/325°F/Gas 3 / Melt the remaining butter in a casserole dish and add the onions and season / Cover and cook on a low heat for 5 minutes / Turn up the heat and add the ground spices and pork / Cook until the pork changes colour, then add the stock / Cover and cook in the oven for 45–60 minutes, or until the pork is tender / While the pork is cooking, heat the olive oil in a hot pan and cook the mushrooms until golden / After the pork has been in the oven for 30 minutes, add the mushrooms / When the pork is cooked, remove the meat and mushrooms from the juices, set aside but keep warm / Add the cream to the juices and boil with the lid off for a few minutes / Slowly whisk in about 2 tablespoons of the roux while the mixture is boiling / Add the parsley, the pork and mushrooms / Season and place in a large pie dish.

Mash
Wash the potatoes, but do not peel them / Place in a saucepan of cold salted water / Bring the water to the boil, cook for 10 minutes then pour out all but about 4cm (1½ inches) of the water and continue to cook the potatoes on a very low heat / About 20 minutes later, test them with a skewer; if they are soft, take them off the heat / Peel the potatoes while they are still hot, holding them in a tea towel / Mash them, adding the butter, and then the boiling milk (or milk and cream) only when they are free of lumps – you may not need it at all depending on the texture of the potatoes / Season to taste / Turn the oven up to 180°C/350°F/Gas 4 / Arrange the mashed potato on top of the filling / Cook in the oven for 30–40 minutes, or until golden brown and bubbling.

Beans
About 15 minutes before the pie is ready, cook the beans by boiling rapidly for 3–4 minutes or until they are just tender / Drain immediately, rinse with cold water and set aside / Heat the oil in a frying pan over a medium heat and add the mustard seeds / As soon as the seeds begin to pop, add the garlic and cook, stirring, until it starts to turn light brown / Add the chilli, stir, then add the green beans, salt and sugar and stir again to mix / Turn the heat to medium-low, stirring the beans for 7–8 minutes / Season with freshly ground black pepper.

To serve

Place some beans on each serving plate and serve a spoonful of the pork and mushroom pie alongside.

Wine expert Olly Smith's choice
Barossa Chardonnay

Si King
Fruit gammon with a spiced marmalade glaze and two zingy salsas

Most people only cook gammon at Christmas, but it's great any time of year.

Ingredients Serves 6

Glaze
4 teaspoons thick-cut marmalade
2 tablespoons honey
1 teaspoon mixed spice
1 teaspoon ground ginger
1 teaspoon freshly ground black pepper

Gammon
3kg (6Ib 6oz) gammon – smoked or unsmoked
1 litre (1¾ pints) pineapple juice
1 litre (1¾ pints) apple juice
2 bay leaves
2 star anise
4 allspice berries
1 apple, halved
1 orange, peeled, pith removed and halved
Zest of 1 lime
1 cinnamon stick
7.5cm (3 inch) piece of fresh root ginger, peeled

Pineapple salsa
1 medium pineapple
½ cucumber, deseeded
½ head of fennel, thinly sliced
1 red chilli, deseeded and finely chopped
4 teaspoons golden caster sugar
2 tablespoons raspberry vinegar

Beetroot and apple salsa
4 cooked beetroot, diced
2 large dessert apples, diced
Zest and juice of 1 lime
4 tablespoons roughly chopped mint leaves

To serve
2 bunches of watercress, leaves picked
Crusty bread

Method

Glaze
Put all the ingredients into a small pan, place on the heat and stir until all the ingredients combine / Simmer for about 5 minutes, stirring all the time, then remove from the heat and set aside.

Gammon
Place the gammon in a large pan and add all the other gammon ingredients / Bring to the boil, then reduce the heat, cover and simmer for 3 hours / When the gammon is cooked, preheat the oven to 180°C/350°F/Gas 4 / Remove the gammon from the pan and place in a roasting tin / Remove the skin, leaving a thick layer of fat / Score the fat all over in a diamond pattern / Brush the glaze all over the gammon, then place in the oven until the glaze caramelises, about 25 minutes / Remove from the oven and set aside to rest / You can reduce the gammon cooking stock to make an additional citrus sauce, if you like / To do this, strain the stock and reduce it until it thickens (about 20 minutes at a simmer) – once thickened you can adjust the sweetness by adding honey if you wish.

Pineapple salsa
While the gammon is in the oven, dice the pineapple and cucumber and mix with the chopped fennel and chilli in a bowl / Put the sugar and vinegar into a saucepan on a medium heat until the sugar dissolves / Pour the vinegar over the salsa and toss everything together.

Beetroot salsa
Once you've made your pineapple salsa, put the beetroot and apples in a bowl and add the lime juice and zest / Add the chopped mint and mix well.

To serve
Put a small handful of watercress in the centre of each serving plate / Carve the gammon and place 2 slices on top of the watercress / Place a spoonful of salsa either side / Serve with crusty bread and a little citrus sauce, if made.

Wine expert Susy Atkins's choice
Torrontés Mendoza
This wine is a bit riper and richer than is usual from Torrontés, but we need that to stand up to this fruity gammon. There's a crisp, fresh finish that will pick up on the lovely elements of the salsas.

Glynn Purnell
Roast loin of pork fillet with carrots cooked in toffee, cumin and passion fruit with smoked salt and borage leaves

Glynn made his reputation from cooking these carrots and you'll easily see why when you try them ...

Ingredients Serves 2

Pork
2 pork tenderloins, trimmed
   and cut in half
1 teaspoon vegetable oil
25g (1oz) butter

Carrots
2 large carrots, peeled
50g (2oz) sugar
25g (1oz) butter
1 rounded teaspoon ground
   cumin
20 baby carrots, trimmed
1 large passion fruit

To serve
½–1 teaspoon smoked
   sea salt
2 punnets of borage shoots
   or cress

Method

Pork
Preheat the oven to 200°C/400°F/Gas 6 / Dry the pork fillets with kitchen towel, but do not season them / Heat an ovenproof frying pan, add the oil and the pork and seal on each side until browned / Add the butter and place in the oven for 6–8 minutes / When cooked, remove from the oven, season the pork with salt and black pepper and set aside to rest.

Carrots
While the pork is cooking, slice the large carrots on a mandolin, or with a vegetable peeler, into wide thin strips / Heat a sauté pan until hot, add the sugar and cook for a couple of minutes until slightly brown / Whisk in the butter and cumin to make a light toffee / Add the carrot ribbons to the toffee, stirring continuously to ensure a complete covering / Leave the carrots to cook in the toffee off the heat / Bring a pan of salted water to the boil, add the baby carrots and cook for 1–2 minutes, until tender but still with a little crunch, then drain and set aside / Scoop out the inside of the passion fruit and stir into the toffee, then add the baby carrots and toss to coat thoroughly / Season to taste.

To serve

Cut the meat in half lengthways and season with the smoked sea salt / Place on serving plates and spoon the carrots over the pork, making sure each plate has plenty of passion fruit seeds / Scatter with the borage leaves.

Wine expert Tim Atkin's choice
Tesco Finest Alsace Pinot Gris
Pinot Gris and Pinot Grigio are exactly the same grape, but the wines are often made in a slightly different style. Pinot Gris tends to be a bit richer, with a little bit more texture to it – this one will go beautifully with the pork.

Matt Tebbutt
Old Spot pork cooked with milk, cinnamon, bay and lemon

Don't be put off by appearances – this is a fabulous dish. The milk will curdle and that's meant to happen. It definitely tastes better than it looks!

Ingredients Serves 4–6

Pork

2–3 kg (4Ib 4oz–6Ib 6oz) Old Spot pork loin, French trimmed, with the chine bone removed
2 tablespoons olive oil
110g (4oz) butter
2 white onions, peeled and cut into quarters
3 garlic bulbs, cut in half
2–2.5 litres (3½–4½ pints) full-fat milk – enough to cover the pork
Zest and juice of 2 lemons
25g (1oz) fresh coriander leaves
4–5 bay leaves
20g (¾oz) cinnamon sticks
10g (½oz) mixed peppercorns
½ nutmeg, freshly grated
5 cloves

Rice

300g (11oz) basmati rice
4 tablespoons roughly chopped fresh flat-leaf parsley
4 tablespoons roughly chopped fresh chives
4 tablespoons roughly chopped fresh coriander

Greens

400g (14oz) selection of spring greens, roughly chopped
50g (2oz) butter

Method

Pork

Preheat the oven to 150°C/300°F/Gas 2 / Season the pork all over with salt and black pepper / Heat a flameproof deep casserole dish (large enough to hold the pork) and add the olive oil and pork / Seal the meat on each side until browned, then leave in the pan, bone side down / Add the butter, onions and garlic and fry for 2–3 minutes more / Add the milk almost to cover, along with the lemon zest, half the juice, the coriander, bay leaves and spices / Place in the oven and cook uncovered for 1½–2 hours, until the bones pull away easily / Remove the pork from the casserole and keep warm / Skim the sauce of excess fat, taste and pour in the remaining lemon juice / Place on the heat, bring to the boil, then simmer until thickened – the sauce should now be nicely curdled.

Rice

About 20 minutes before the pork is due to come out of the oven, bring a pan of salted water to the boil / Add the rice and cook for 12–14 minutes, until tender / Drain and return the rice to the pan to drive off any excess moisture / Season with salt and black pepper, then add the herbs and toss to combine.

Greens

While the rice is cooking, bring a separate pan of salted water to the boil / Add the greens and cook for 2–3 minutes, until just tender / Drain, return to the pan, and add the butter and some salt and black pepper.

To serve

Remove the bones from the pork, then cut the meat into slices and place on serving plates / Spoon over the sauce, including the softened onions and cinnamon sticks, and pile some greens and herbed rice alongside.

Wine expert Olly Smith's choice
Anakena Single Vineyard Viognier
This is a white wine with a round texture and an aromatic edge to seduce the spices. There's a real fragrance to the aroma of this one, and some people say it smells like apricots.

Martin Blunos
Boiled collar of bacon with veggies and dumplings

This is a cheap, tasty alternative to a traditional Sunday roast. You can use the cooking liquor and any leftover ham to make a great soup the following day.

Ingredients Serves 4

Bacon
1.35kg (3lb) collar of bacon, skin on, soaked in plenty of cold water (overnight at least)
1 fresh bay leaf
10 black peppercorns
2 cloves
1 stick cinnamon
1 large onion, peeled
570ml (1 pint) good cider
25g (1oz) butter
4 large garlic cloves, peeled
8 small shallots, peeled but with root end intact
10 white peppercorns
4 medium carrots, sliced on the diagonal 5mm (¼ inch) thick
3 sticks celery, sliced on the diagonal 5mm (¼ inch) thick

Dumplings
90g (3½oz) self-raising flour
1 teaspoon English mustard powder
45g (1¾oz) shredded suet
1 heaped tablespoon chopped fresh parsley

To serve

English mustard

Method

Bacon
Remove the bacon joint from the soaking water and put it into a large deep saucepan / Add the bay leaf, black peppercorns, cloves, cinnamon, onion and cider and pour in enough cold water to cover the joint by a good 2.5cm (1 inch) / Cover and bring to the boil, then reduce to a simmer / Cook for 1 hour, then test with a blunt knife to see if the meat is tender – if it's still a bit difficult to insert the blade, continue cooking for another 20 minutes then test again / Remove the pan from the heat and set aside / Preheat the oven to 190°C/375°F/Gas 5 / Heat a large casserole, add the butter, garlic, shallots and white peppercorns and cook for 1 minute / Add the carrots and celery and cook gently for about 5 minutes to give them a little colour / Remove the bacon from the poaching liquor / Cut and lift off the skin – it should come off in an even sheet / Put the skinned bacon on top of the vegetables in the casserole and add enough of the poaching liquor to cover the vegetables by 2.5cm (1 inch) / Cover with a lid and place in the oven for 15 minutes.

Dumplings
While the bacon is cooking in the oven, sift the flour, mustard powder and a good pinch of salt into a bowl / Mix in the suet, parsley and plenty of black pepper and add enough cold water to make a stiffish dough that won't cling to the sides of the bowl / Divide into large walnut-sized pieces and roll into neat balls / When the bacon has had its final 15 minutes in the oven, add the dumplings to the casserole, around the joint, and put back into the oven for a further 25–30 minutes / When done, the dumplings should be cooked through, puffed and light, the meat will be tender, the vegetables will have collapsed a little and be bursting with flavour, and the cooking liquor will have thickened slightly into a sauce.

To serve

Carefully lift the meat from the casserole on to a board and cut into generous slices / Place a bed of the vegetables on each serving plate, top with slices of bacon, add a few dumplings and finally spoon over the sauce from the casserole / Serve with English mustard.

Wine expert Olly Smith's choice
Sainsbury's Taste the Difference Chenin Blanc
This has got the crunch of an apple and the zing of a lemon, which will work so well with the bacon. It's got a roundness of texture from being partially fermented in oak barrels.

James Martin
Spiced pot-roasted pork loin with sautéd potatoes and roasted carrots

Juniper berries, which are used to flavour gin, give this recipe a wonderful aromatic twist.

Ingredients Serves 6

Pork

1.5kg (3lb 4oz) pork loin
3 Bramley apples, peeled, cored and cut into chunks
½ teaspoon ground cinnamon
¼ teaspoon ground allspice
3 star anise
1 teaspoon cloves
1 teaspoon juniper berries
50g (2oz) butter, diced
150ml (5fl oz) of water

Carrots

300g (11oz) baby carrots, scrubbed
25g (1oz) butter
2 tablespoons honey

Potatoes

25g (1oz) butter
3 tablespoons olive oil
4 potatoes, peeled and cut into thick slices

Method

Pork

Preheat the oven to 190°C/375°F/Gas 5 / Score the fat on the pork and rub with a little salt and black pepper / Place the apples in the bottom of an ovenproof lidded dish / Scatter over the cinnamon, allspice, star anise, cloves and juniper berries and toss to combine / Sprinkle over the butter and add the water / Place the pork on top and cover with the lid / Put in the oven for 1 hour, then remove the lid and turn the heat up to 220°C/425°F/Gas 7 / Cook for a further 45 minutes, until the fat is crispy and the meat cooked through / Remove from the oven and set aside to rest for 15 minutes, leaving the oven on.

Carrots

While the meat is resting, place the carrots in a small roasting tray, add the butter and dot with the honey / Place in the oven for 5–8 minutes.

Potatoes

While the carrots are in the oven, heat a frying pan and add the butter, olive oil and potatoes / Fry the potatoes over a medium heat until golden brown and tender – about 4–5 minutes / Season with salt and black pepper.

To serve

Carve the pork into thick slices and place on serving plates / Place a spoonful of the puréed apples on top of the pork / Spoon the potatoes and carrots alongside.

Wine expert Susy Atkins's choice
Marks & Spencer Australian Shiraz

Matt Tebbutt
Rump of salt marsh lamb, rock samphire and broad beans, with balsamic meat juices and persillade

Lawrence Keogh
Lamb rasher salad

Martin Blunos
Lamb steaks with anchovy butter, salsify and walnuts

Mark Sargeant
Pan-fried lamb cutlets with marjoram crushed peas, tomatoes and anchovy dressing

James Martin
Sage-stuffed lamb chops with Serrano ham and sage pasta

Madhur Jaffrey
Lamb shanks braised in a yoghurt sauce with basmati pilaf, dill and cardamom

Donna Hay
Prosciutto-wrapped lamb cutlets with green beans and crunchy parsnip ribbons

James Martin
Slow-roasted shoulder of hogget with lemon, rosemary, onion mash and roasted parsnips

Galton Blackiston
Slowly braised breast of lamb with artichoke purée and sprouting broccoli

James Martin
Roasted crown of lamb with Dauphinoise potatoes, steamed vegetables and mint sauce

Bryn Williams
Lamb stew with rosemary dumplings

James Martin
Sautéd kidneys with mash

Lamb

Matt Tebbutt
Rump of salt marsh lamb, rock samphire and broad beans, with balsamic meat juices and persillade

Rock samphire is a true forager's ingredient as it grows hundreds of feet up on the side of cliffs; harvesting is best left to the experts!

Ingredients Serves 4

Lamb and samphire
2 tablespoons olive oil
4 x 225g (8oz) rump of salt marsh lamb
110g (4oz) butter
200g (7oz) rock samphire
175g (6oz) double-shelled young broad beans
2 tablespoons balsamic vinegar
2 tablespoons lamb or veal stock

Persillade
1 banana shallot, finely diced
1 garlic clove, finely chopped
3 tablespoons roughly chopped fresh flat-leaf parsley

Method

Lamb and samphire
Preheat the oven to 200°C/400°F/Gas 6 / Heat an ovenproof frying pan, add the olive oil and the lamb, skin side down, and cook for 2–3 minutes on each side / Place in the oven and cook for 12–15 minutes / Remove from the oven and place the lamb on a plate, reserving the pan for later / Meanwhile, heat a second frying pan and add 25g (1oz) of the butter and the rock samphire / Sauté for 2 minutes, until just wilted / Add the broad beans and toss to combine / Season with salt and black pepper / Take the frying pan the meat was cooked in, drain off the meat juices and reserve, then return the pan to the heat / Add the balsamic vinegar, bring to the boil and stir, deglazing the pan / Add the lamb or veal stock and simmer for 1 minute / Add the remaining butter and swirl to combine / Pour the meat juices back into the pan and bring to a simmer / Season with salt and black pepper.

Persillade
Place the shallot, garlic and parsley in a bowl and toss to combine.

To serve

Slice the lamb thickly and arrange on a serving dish / Place the rock samphire alongside, then pour the sauce over the lamb and scatter the persillade over the top.

Wine expert Tim Atkin's choice
Sainsbury's Taste the Difference Côtes du Rhône Villages
You've got to serve a red wine with this dish, but there's one challenging ingredient, the rock samphire. Those salty, tangy flavours don't work well with red wines that are tannic, so I'm going for something that's soft but full-bodied.

Lawrence Keogh
Lamb rasher salad

This is typical Lawrence, British to the core, seasonal and unique. But it's best to get your dandelions from your fruit and vegetable supplier, not the hard shoulder!

Ingredients Serves 4

Lamb
1 lamb belly, approx 1.35kg (3Ib)

Dressing
150ml (5fl oz) rapeseed oil
50ml (2fl oz) Cabernet Sauvignon red wine vinegar

Salad
125g (4½oz) wild garlic leaves
2 dandelion bunches, washed
20g (1¾oz) bull's blood leaves, washed
8 spring onions, thinly sliced at an angle
75g (3oz) capers, drained and dried
40 fresh mint leaves cut into fine strips

Method

Lamb
Preheat the oven to 170°C/325°F/Gas 3 / Season the lamb with salt and black pepper, place in a roasting tin and cook in the oven for 2½ hours / Remove from the oven and, while still warm, pull the bones away from the lamb / Lay the cooked meat between sheets of greaseproof paper, press between 2 trays and chill for a few hours or overnight / Preheat the grill to medium / Slice the cooked lamb thinly and place on a tray under a warm grill or in a hot oven for 5–6 minutes.

Dressing and salad
Stir the oil and vinegar together – do not whisk / Place all the salad leaves in a bowl with the spring onions / Heat a small frying pan and add enough sunflower or vegetable oil to cover by 1cm, then heat until medium hot / Add the capers and deep-fry for 30–45 seconds, then drain on kitchen paper.

To serve

Toss the warm lamb through the leaves along with the mint / Add the dressing, season and serve sprinkled with the deep-fried capers.

Wine expert Susy Atkins's choice
Porta Cabernet Sauvignon Carmenere
Cabernet Sauvignon grapes have been blended here with Chile's Carmenere to make a particularly soft, ripe and juicy wine. It's all raspberries and redcurrants oozing out of the glass, soft and very rounded on the finish.

Martin Blunos
Lamb steaks with anchovy butter, salsify and walnuts

Anchovies are a wonderful accompaniment to lamb. They dissolve in the cooking process, and even if you think you don't like them you'll enjoy their effect on the meat.

Ingredients Serves 2

Lamb
2 tablespoons olive oil
1 garlic clove, peeled and crushed
2 x 225g (8oz) leg of lamb steaks

Anchovy butter
250g (9oz) butter, at room temperature
1 teaspoon anchovy essence
Zest of 1 lemon
6 anchovies, drained of oil and chopped

Salsify
750g (1lb 10oz) salsify
2 lemons
25g (1oz) plain flour
1.5 litres (2½ pints) cold water
1 teaspoon salt
1 tablespoon clarified butter
75g (3oz) walnut halves
1 tablespoon sultanas, soaked overnight in enough brandy to cover
½ teaspoon caster sugar
1 tablespoon sherry vinegar
25g (1oz) butter
1 tablespoon walnut oil

To serve

2 tablespoons fresh flat-leaf parsley leaves

Method

Lamb
Massage the oil and garlic into the lamb steaks, put them into a bowl, cover and place in the fridge for at least 6 hours / Just before cooking, remove the meat from the fridge and bring back to room temperature / Heat a griddle pan, then lift the steak out of the oil and place on the griddle for 3-4 minutes on each side / Remove to a heatproof dish and season with salt and black pepper.

Anchovy butter
While the lamb steaks are marinating in the fridge, place the butter in a bowl, add the anchovy essence, lemon zest and anchovies and mix well / Place on a piece of clingfilm or baking parchment and roll into a log / Put into the fridge and chill until firm.

Salsify
Before you start to cook the lamb, peel the salsify and cut it into 5cm (2 inch) pieces / Put it immediately into a bowl of water with the juice of 1 lemon / Put the flour into a saucepan and add a little of the water, stirring to make a smooth paste / Add the rest of the water, the salt and the juice of the second lemon to form a blanc / Bring to the boil, whisking to prevent the pan catching / Drain the salsify and place in the blanc, bring to the boil, then reduce the heat to a simmer and cook for 15 minutes, until the salsify is tender / Drain and rinse in cold water, then pat dry / Heat a non-stick frying pan and add half the clarified butter followed by the salsify / Season with a little salt and black pepper and fry gently to colour and heat through / Place the remaining clarified butter in another frying pan, add the walnuts and place over a high heat for a couple of minutes / Add the sultanas, sugar and vinegar / Remove from the heat, whisk in the remaining butter and walnut oil, and season with salt and black pepper / Pour over the salsify and toss together.

To serve

Slice the anchovy butter and place on top of the lamb steaks / Flash in a hot oven or under a grill to melt / Place on serving plates, spoon the salsify alongside and finish with a scattering of parsley leaves.

Wine expert Olly Smith's choice
Mirambelo
The bitterness of the salsify and the savoury tang of the walnuts are going to pick up brilliantly on the oak ageing that this wine has had. It delivers just enough poke to make the perfect match.

Mark Sargeant
Pan-fried lamb cutlets with marjoram crushed peas, tomatoes and anchovy dressing

Mark's idea for serving peas is great and works well with most meats or fish.

Ingredients Serves 4

Lamb

12 lamb cutlets, trimmed
1 tablespoon olive oil
2 garlic cloves, lightly crushed
2 sprigs of fresh rosemary
6 anchovies
12 small tomatoes, cut into quarters
12 black olives, cut in half
2 tablespoons extra virgin olive oil
2 tablespoons good red wine vinegar
1 tablespoon fresh marjoram leaves

Peas

25g (1oz) butter
300g (11oz) fresh peas, blanched
2 tablespoons fresh marjoram leaves
2 tablespoons crème fraîche

Method

Lamb

Season the lamb cutlets with salt and black pepper / Heat a frying pan and add the olive oil, lamb, garlic, rosemary and 2 of the anchovies / Fry the lamb on each side for 2–3 minutes, until golden, then remove from the pan to a plate and set aside / Add the tomatoes, olives and remaining chopped anchovies to the pan and sauté for 2 minutes / Add the extra virgin olive oil and vinegar and whisk to combine / Season with a little salt and black pepper, then add the marjoram leaves and stir.

Peas

While the lamb is cooking, heat a frying pan, add the butter, peas and marjoram and sauté for 2 minutes, until the peas are hot and cooked through / Using a potato masher, crush the peas lightly / Add the crème fraîche and mix well / Season with salt and black pepper.

To serve

Pile some of the peas into the centre of each serving plate and top with 3 cutlets / Spoon the tomato dressing around the edge of the plates.

Wine expert Olly Smith's choice
Tinto da Anfora Alentejano
This wine is made by hand from local grape varieties. It's complex, balanced and delicious. It has a silky texture, and the salty twist in this dish will pick up beautifully on the hint of spice and vanilla in the wine.

James Martin
Sage-stuffed lamb chops with Serrano ham and sage pasta

The Italians use sage a lot and see it as a really versatile herb. Lamb and sage is a great combination.

Ingredients Serves 4

Pasta
550g (1lb 4oz) 'OO' pasta flour, plus extra for dusting
4 whole eggs
5 egg yolks
50g (2oz) butter
6 fresh sage leaves, finely chopped

Lamb
12 French-trimmed lamb chops
12 fresh sage leaves
6 slices Serrano ham
50g (2oz) butter
4 tablespoons vegetable oil

Method

Pasta
Place the flour in a large bowl, then make a well in the centre, crack in the whole eggs and add the egg yolks / Mix well until the dough comes together as a ball, then knead, using your hands, for about 5 minutes / Cover and allow to rest for as long as possible, then cut into portions and freeze any extra / Flour the pasta machine – starting at the lowest (thickest) setting, feed a portion of the dough through the machine, turning the handle with one hand and holding the dough as it comes through the machine with the other / Change the setting on the pasta machine to the next-thickest setting, flour it again and feed the pasta sheet through again, as before / Repeat this process 3 or 4 more times, flouring the machine and turning the setting down each time (any pasta you are not working on should be covered with clingfilm to prevent it drying out) / Finish running the pasta through on the tagliatelle cutter / Bring a large pan of salted water to the boil / Add the pasta, cook for 2–3 minutes, then drain and toss in the butter and the chopped sage.

Lamb
While the water for the pasta is coming to the boil, cut a little pocket into the side of each lamb chop and press half a sage leaf and a little piece of Serrano ham inside / Season the chops with salt and black pepper, then wrap with the remaining Serrano ham / Heat a frying pan, add the butter and the chops and fry in batches on each side for 3–4 minutes, until cooked through / Meanwhile, heat the oil in a small frying pan, add the remaining sage leaves and fry for 1 minute until crispy / Drain on kitchen paper.

To serve

Pile some pasta on to each serving plate / Place 3 chops alongside and finish with the fried sage leaves.

Madhur Jaffrey
Lamb shanks braised in a yoghurt sauce with basmati pilaf, dill and cardamom

This dish is one of Madhur's classics and is wonderfully light with the yoghurt sauce; you'll want to cook it again and again.

Ingredients Serves 4

Lamb shanks

4 lamb shanks
2 teaspoons salt
13cm (5 inch) piece of fresh root ginger, peeled and roughly chopped
8 garlic cloves, peeled and roughly chopped
525ml (18fl oz) water
4 teaspoons coriander seeds
8 teaspoons olive or corn oil
2 teaspoons cumin seeds
1 teaspoon whole cloves
4 medium cinnamon sticks
2 teaspoons black peppercorns
500g (16oz) natural yoghurt, lightly beaten until smooth
1½ teaspoons coarsely ground chilli powder or cayenne pepper
½ teaspoon ground turmeric

Rice

500g (16oz) measure of basmati rice
3 tablespoons corn, peanut or olive oil
1 medium cinnamon stick
5 cardamom pods
2 bay leaves
90g (3½oz) onion, sliced into fine half-rings
25g (1oz) fresh dill, finely chopped
650ml (1¼ pints) chicken stock

Method

Lamb shanks

Preheat the oven to 170°C/325°F/Gas 3 / Place the lamb shanks in a single layer and sprinkle all over with ½ teaspoon of the salt and lots of pepper, patting them in / Put the ginger and garlic into a blender with 4 tablespoons of the water and blend until smooth, then set aside / Put the coriander seeds in a clean coffee grinder and grind coarsely (or you can use a mortar and pestle), then set aside / Pour the oil into a wide, ovenproof, lidded pan and set over a high heat / When hot, add the lamb shanks and brown lightly on all sides / Remove the lamb shanks from the pan and quickly add the cumin, cloves, cinnamon and peppercorns to the hot oil / Ten seconds later, add the ginger-garlic paste, stir, and fry for 5–6 minutes or until lightly browned / Take the pan off the heat, add the beaten yoghurt and the remaining water and stir well / Put the pan back on the heat; add the coarsely ground coriander seeds, chilli powder, turmeric and the remaining 1½ teaspoons of salt, and stir / Put the lamb shanks back into the pan, spoon some of the sauce over them, and bring to the boil / Cover well, first with foil, crimping the edges, then with the lid, and place in the oven to bake slowly for 3 hours, turning the shanks over every 30 minutes / Remove the pan from the oven and take off the lid / Set over a high heat and reduce the liquid, basting the shanks as you do so, until you have a thick sauce, about 6–7 minutes.

Rice

About an hour before the lamb shanks are due to be ready, put the rice into a bowl and wash in several changes of water / Drain, add fresh water to cover generously, leave to soak for 30 minutes, then drain / Pour the oil into a heavy, lidded pan that will just hold the cooked rice comfortably and set it over a medium heat / When the oil is hot, add the cinnamon stick, cardamom and bay leaves / Stir for 5 seconds then add the onions and stir-fry until they turn reddish-brown / Add the rice and dill, reduce the heat to medium low, and stir for about 2 minutes until the rice grains look translucent / Add the stock and bring to the boil / Cover the pan tightly, reduce the heat to very, very low and cook for 25 minutes.

To serve

Pile the rice on to serving plates and spoon the lamb shanks alongside.

Wine expert Olly Smith's choice
Maycas del Limari Syrah Reserva
For this dish you need a wine that's ripe, deep, juicy and a whole barrel of fun. This one has a juicy, soft texture and is like getting your nose into a bathtub of blackberries!

Donna Hay
Prosciutto-wrapped lamb cutlets with green beans and crunchy parsnip ribbons

Don't take your eyes off the parsnip ribbons while they're cooking – they burn quite easily, as we found out on the show!

Ingredients Serves 4

Lamb
110g (4oz) quince paste
4 x 125g (4½oz) lamb double cutlets, trimmed
8 slices prosciutto
2 tablespoons olive oil
175g (6oz) green beans, trimmed
175g (6oz) butter beans
250ml (9fl oz) hot chicken stock
75ml (3fl oz) dry white wine
25g (1oz) butter

Parsnip ribbons
4 x 150g (5oz) parsnips
60g (2½oz) butter, melted
2 tablespoons brown sugar

Method

Lamb
Preheat the oven to 200°C/400°F/Gas 6 / Spread 1 teaspoon of quince paste over each side of the lamb cutlets and sprinkle with salt and pepper / Wrap each cutlet with 2 slices of prosciutto and brush with olive oil / Heat a large non-stick frying pan and cook the lamb for 30 seconds each side or until browned, then set aside / Arrange the green beans and butter beans in a 35cm x 23cm (14 x 9 inch) ceramic baking dish / Pour over the stock and wine and dot with butter / Place the lamb on top of the beans and roast for 10 minutes for medium rare or until it is cooked to your liking.

Parsnip ribbons
Use a vegetable peeler to cut the parsnips into long thin strips / Place on a baking tray lined with non-stick baking parchment and toss with the butter, sugar and some salt / Roast with the lamb for 10 minutes, tossing and separating the parsnips as much as you can, then return them to the oven and cook for a further 8–10 minutes or until golden and crunchy.

To serve

Place the lamb and beans on serving plates and serve the parsnip ribbons alongside.

Wine expert Olly Smith's choice
Wakefield Cabernet Sauvignon
Lamb has a natural sweetness to it, and for me Cabernet Sauvignon from the New World just does it so many favours. The tangy, salty quality in the prosciutto is going to work brilliantly with the acidity in this wine.

James Martin
Slow-roasted shoulder of hogget with lemon, rosemary, onion mash and roasted parsnips

Hogget is one-year old lamb. As it is a little older, it has a much richer flavour but is still tender and utterly mouth-watering. You can use lamb instead, if you prefer.

Ingredients Serves 6–8

Hogget
4kg (7½lb) shoulder of hogget
Zest of 2 lemons
3 sprigs of fresh rosemary, leaves picked and finely chopped
1 teaspoon sea salt
2 star anise, crushed
2 tablespoons olive oil

Onion mash
110g (4oz) butter
2 onions, roughly chopped
300ml (10fl oz) white wine
300ml (10fl oz) double cream
1kg (2lb 2oz) floury potatoes, peeled and cut into chunks

Parsnips
50g (2oz) butter
2 tablespoons olive oil
6 parsnips, peeled and quartered
2 tablespoons honey

Method

Hogget
Preheat the oven to 150°C/300°F/Gas 2 / Place the hogget in a roasting tin / Mix together the lemon zest, rosemary, salt, star anise and oil in a bowl and rub into the meat / Place in the oven for at least 3 hours, preferably 5, basting with the juices from the bottom of the pan, until the meat falls away from the bone / Remove from the oven and set aside to rest.

Onion mash
Half an hour before the hogget is due to be ready, heat a frying pan, add the butter and the onions and cook over a low heat until softened / Add the white wine and cream and bring to a simmer / Cook for 10–12 minutes, until the onions are very soft and the cream has reduced down by half / Season with salt and black pepper, then place in a blender or food processor and blitz to a purée / Transfer the purée to a clean pan / Meanwhile, bring a pan of salted water to the boil, add the potatoes and cook for 15 minutes, until tender / Drain and return to the pan over the heat to drive off any excess moisture / Pass through a potato ricer and add to the onion purée / Mix well and reheat – adjusting the seasoning if necessary.

Parsnips
While the hogget is resting, turn up the oven to 200°C/400°F/Gas 6 / Heat a frying pan, add the butter, oil and parsnips and fry on each side until just golden / Add the honey, salt and black pepper and toss well, then transfer to an ovenproof dish or a roasting tin and place in the oven for 20–25 minutes until tender.

To serve

Pile the onion mash into the centre of the plate, with a pile of parsnips to one side / Arrange the hogget to the side of the mash and spoon over any juices left at the bottom of the pan.

Wine expert Peter Richards's choice
Cono Sur Merlot Reserva

Galton Blackiston
Slowly braised breast of lamb with artichoke purée and sprouting broccoli

Ask your butcher to do the hard work of tying up the lamb so that all you have to do is place it in the oven and go fishing for a couple of hours, just like Galton ...

Ingredients Serves 4–6

Lamb

1 tablespoon olive oil
25g (1oz) butter
1.25kg (2lb 11oz) breast of lamb, taken off the bone, rolled and tied
1 onion, chopped
2 carrots, chopped
1 leek, chopped
½ head of garlic, chopped
1 sprig of fresh rosemary
1.2 litres (2 pints) chicken or vegetable stock
2 tablespoons double cream
3 tablespoons superfine capers
3 tablespoons roughly chopped fresh flat-leaf parsley

Artichokes and broccoli

450g (1lb) Jerusalem artichokes, peeled and cut into chunks
½ lemon
25g (1oz) butter
25ml (1fl oz) double cream
Pinch of freshly ground nutmeg
300g (11oz) sprouting broccoli

Method

Lamb

Preheat the oven to 150°C/300°F/Gas 3 / Heat a frying pan, add the oil followed by the butter and allow to foam / Add the lamb and brown all over, then season the meat and remove to a plate / In the same frying pan, just colour the vegetables, garlic and rosemary, and put them into a large casserole dish, placing the lamb on top / Warm the stock to just below a simmer then pour it over the lamb / Put a lid on top, place in the oven and braise the lamb for 3–4 hours, until tender / Leave the lamb to cool completely in the stock, preferably overnight / The next day, remove the lamb from the stock, carve into thick slices and place in a roasting tin / Warm the stock and pour some of it over the lamb and put the rest in a pan / Cover the lamb with foil and keep warm / Now bring the stock in the pan to the boil and reduce by at least half, tasting as you go / Strain, then return it to the pan and add the cream / Simmer to reduce a little more, then add the capers and parsley.

Artichokes and broccoli

Half an hour or so before you are ready to serve the lamb, place the artichokes in a saucepan of cold salted water. Squeeze in the juice of the lemon half then add the lemon half to the pan, bring to the boil and cook until very soft (about 15–20 minutes) / Drain, then remove the lemon and place the artichokes in a blender or food processor with the butter and cream / Blitz until very smooth, then adjust the seasoning with salt, pepper and a little grated nutmeg / Heat a pan of salted water until boiling, drop in the broccoli and boil for about 3 minutes, until just tender / Drain and season with salt and black pepper.

To serve

If you like, you can fry the lamb slices in a little butter just before serving / Spoon the artichoke purée on to serving plates and top with 3 pieces of broccoli / Carefully lift the lamb slices and put them beside the vegetables / Finally spoon the sauce over the meat.

Wine expert Tim Atkin's choice
île La Forge Merlot
Artichokes are always a challenge for wine matching. This wine has lovely notes of vanilla and coffee bean on the nose, and on the palate there are some tannins there, which will match the rusticity of the dish. This is a really good wine to serve with lamb.

James Martin
Roasted crown of lamb with Dauphinoise potatoes, steamed vegetables and mint sauce

The crown cut makes this surprisingly simple dish look really impressive. And nothing enhances lamb like a good mint sauce.

Ingredients Serves 4

Dauphinoise potatoes
50g (2oz) butter, softened
1–1.25kg (2Ib 2oz–2Ib 11oz) white potatoes, peeled and thinly sliced
2 garlic cloves, finely chopped
250ml (9fl oz) full-fat milk
250ml (9fl oz) double cream

Lamb and vegetables
1–1.25kg (2Ib 2oz–2Ib 11oz) crown of lamb, fully trimmed
400g (14oz) broccoli florets
200g (7oz) fine green beans, trimmed
175g (6oz) baby carrots, trimmed

Mint sauce
6 tablespoons cider vinegar
1½ tablespoons caster sugar
5 tablespoons finely chopped fresh mint leaves

Method

Dauphinoise potatoes
Preheat the oven to 170°C/325°F/Gas 3 / Butter a medium-size ovenproof dish with half the butter and place in a deep oven tray / Layer the potatoes into the dish, sprinkling with garlic, salt and black pepper several times throughout the layers / Combine the milk and cream and pour over the potatoes, adding as much of it as you can – the potatoes should be just covered / Dot with the remaining butter and cover the dish with foil / Place the roasting tray in the oven and cook for 1½ hours, until just tender – check halfway through and, if necessary, add more of the milk and cream mixture / Remove the foil and return to the oven for a further 30 minutes, until the top is golden and the potatoes are tender when pierced with a knife / If you don't have a double oven, cover the potatoes and keep warm until the lamb is cooked, and then return to the oven to heat through while the lamb rests.

Lamb and vegetables
Preheat the oven to 200°C/400°F/Gas 6 / Season the lamb with salt and black pepper and place in a roasting tin / Place in the oven and cook for 25–35 minutes, depending how you like your lamb cooked / Remove from the oven and set aside to rest for 10 minutes / Bring a pan of water to the boil, place a steamer over the top then add the vegetables and cover with a lid / Steam for 5–8 minutes until just tender.

Mint sauce
When the lamb and potatoes are almost ready, place the vinegar and sugar into a saucepan and bring to a simmer / Put the mint into a bowl, pour over the vinegar and stir well / Leave to marinate for a few minutes before serving.

To serve
Carve the lamb into 2-bone pieces and place 2 on each serving plate / Pile the vegetables alongside, with a large spoonful of dauphinoise potatoes / Finish with a drizzle of mint sauce.

Wine expert Olly Smith's choice
Vega Ariana Rioja

Bryn Williams
Lamb stew with rosemary dumplings

If you think dumplings are boring, Bryn's will certainly change your mind – they're the ultimate comfort food for even the coldest winter.

Ingredients Serves 4

Lamb stew
750g (1lb 10oz) lamb neck fillet, cut into 2.5cm (1 inch) cubes
25g (1oz) plain flour
1 tablespoon olive oil
50g (2oz) butter
12 baby onions, peeled
2 medium carrots, cut into large dice
1 medium swede, cut into large dice
50ml (2fl oz) white wine
1.2 litres (2 pints) lamb stock
4 bay leaves
2 sprigs of fresh rosemary

Dumplings
125g (5oz) plain flour
60g (2½ oz) suet
½ teaspoon baking powder
1 tablespoon finely chopped fresh rosemary leaves
3–5 tablespoons cold water
500ml (18fl oz) lamb stock

To serve

3 tablespoons roughly chopped fresh flat-leaf parsley

Method

Lamb stew
Preheat the oven to 130°C/250°F/Gas ½ / Season the lamb with salt and pepper and dust with the flour / Heat a heavy-bottomed casserole, add the olive oil and butter, then add the lamb and fry on each side until golden brown / Remove the lamb to a plate and set aside / Reduce the heat, add the onions, carrots and swede and cook until caramelised / Add the wine and simmer until reduced by half, then add the lamb and the lamb stock / Bring to a simmer, add the bay leaves and rosemary and cover with a lid / Place in the oven for 1 hour.

Dumplings
While the stew is cooking, put the flour, suet, baking powder and a pinch of salt into a bowl / Mix, then add the rosemary and enough cold water to form a sticky dough / Flour your hands and roll the dough into 12 little balls, then place them on a plate in the fridge to chill / When the lamb is ready, bring the lamb stock to a simmer in a large pan / Add the dumplings and simmer for 6–8 minutes / Remove the dumplings with a slotted spoon and set aside to rest for a minute, discarding the cooking stock.

To serve

When the lamb stew is ready, remove the lid and add the dumplings and parsley to the casserole / Serve in individual shallow bowls.

Wine expert Olly Smith's choice
Romeral Rioja Crianza
Red Rioja is predominantly made from the Tempranillo grape. 'Tempranillo' means ripening early, and what that gives you is lots of soft fruit in your glass. The fruit will pick up beautifully on the natural buttery quality of the lamb.

James Martin
Sautéd kidneys with mash

Kidneys are not very fashionable but they're very tasty, cheap and full of goodness, so give them a go ...

Ingredients Serves 4

Mash
300g (11oz) King Edward potatoes, peeled and cut into chunks
50g (2oz) butter
110ml (4fl oz) double cream

Kidneys
50g (2oz) butter
300g (11oz) lamb's kidneys, cleaned and trimmed
2 shallots, sliced
75g (3oz) button onions, peeled
150g (5oz) wild mushrooms
50ml (2fl oz) brandy
90ml (3½fl oz) chicken stock
90ml (3½fl oz) double cream
2 teaspoons wholegrain mustard
3 tablespoons roughly chopped fresh flat-leaf parsley

Method

Mash
Place the potatoes in a pan of salted water, bring to the boil and simmer for 15 minutes, until tender / Drain and return to the pan, over the heat, to drive off any excess moisture / Mash well, then add the butter and cream and beat to a smooth purée / Season with salt and black pepper and keep warm.

Kidneys
Heat a frying pan, add the butter and the kidneys and sauté for 2–3 minutes, until golden / Remove from the pan and set aside / Add the shallots and button onions and cook for 1–2 minutes / Add the wild mushrooms and cook for a further minute / Add the brandy and flambé, then add the stock, bring to a simmer and cook for 1 minute / Add the cream, mustard and kidneys and simmer for 2 minutes, then season with salt and black pepper / Add the parsley and stir well.

To serve

Spoon the mash into the centre of each serving plate and spoon over the kidneys.

James Martin
Leek and smoked salmon tart with salad

Michel Roux
Smoked haddock soufflé

Lawrence Keogh
Poached sea trout with vanilla salad cream, heritage tomatoes and samphire

Jun Tanaka
Red mullet with almonds, escabeche and butternut purée

Rick Stein
Seared swordfish steaks with salmoriglio, tomato and pepper

Matthew Fort
Sgombro alla griglia con capperi e bobbia

Atul Kochhar
Vava meen roast (South Indian fish sandwich)

Vivek Singh
Grilled mackerel fillets with cloves, fennel, pepper and cinnamon, yoghurt kadhi and curry leaf spinach poriyal

Patrick Williams
Roast red bream with fried plantain fritters and coconut sauce

John Torode
Brill en papillote

Nic Watt
Sea bream marinated in ryotei miso with pickled onion salsa

Paul Rankin
Sesame-fried brill with soy mustard vinaigrette, Asian coleslaw and wontons

Michael Caines
Pan-fried grey mullet with a stir-fry of mangetout, shiitake mushrooms and lemongrass sauce

James Martin
Halibut with lychee, cashew nut and miso salad

Nic Watt
Crispy lemon sole with chilli, sesame and soy

Rick Stein
Fish tacos from Baja Califonia with guacamole

Ken Hom
Stir-fried salmon with lemon and basmati rice

Jason Atherton
Tuna with a soy, ginger and chilli glaze with bok choi

James Martin
Roasted dover sole with caper butter, sautéd broad beans and potatoes

James Tanner
Pan-fried fillet of sea bass, sautéd baby gem with prawn and chorizo cassoulet

Fish

Marcus Wareing
Sea trout with liquorice carrots, sautéd baby gem and bisque

Dave Myers
Poached turbot with a lemon and kelp crust, served with a white wine and broad bean sauce on a bed of truffled wild mushrooms with crispy hasselback potatoes

Marcus Wareing
Roasted monkfish and chorizo hotpot

James Tanner
Smoked haddock and leek risotto with poached egg and mustard sauce

Lawrence Keogh
Pan-roasted ling with clams, perry and curly kale

James Martin
Leek and smoked salmon tart with salad

You might not think of cooking with smoked salmon, but it intensifies the flavour of this tart, which is utterly delicious.

Ingredients Serves 6

Tart
500g (1lb 2oz) shortcrust pastry
50g (2oz) butter
750g (1lb 10oz) leeks, finely sliced
5 sprigs of fresh thyme, leaves picked
200ml (7fl oz) double cream
1 egg
1 egg yolk
200g (7oz) smoked salmon
75g (3oz) Gruyère cheese, grated

Salad
1 tablespoon wholegrain mustard
1 tablespoon white wine vinegar
3 tablespoons extra virgin olive oil
2 heads of little gem lettuce, leaves separated
50g (2oz) watercress

Method

Tart
Preheat the oven to 200°C/400°F/Gas 6 / On a lightly floured surface, roll out the pastry and use to line a 20cm (8 inch) diameter, 2.5cm (1 inch) deep loose-bottomed tart tin / Cover and place in the fridge for 30 minutes / Line the pastry tart case with greaseproof paper and fill with baking beans / Bake in the oven for 15 minutes / Remove the greaseproof paper and beans and return the tart case to the oven for a further 5 minutes, until it is just cooked / Reduce the heat to 180°C/350°F/Gas 4 / Meanwhile, heat a large sauté pan, add the butter, leeks and thyme and cook until just softened and all the liquid is cooked away / Remove from the heat and cool / Place the cream, egg and egg yolk in a bowl and whisk / Pour over the cold leeks and mix together, then season with salt and black pepper / Pour into the cooked pastry case / Lay the smoked salmon over the top of the leeks, taking care to cover to the edges / Sprinkle the grated Gruyère over the top of the salmon / Place in the oven for 20 minutes, until just set and the top is golden.

Salad
Whisk the mustard, vinegar and olive oil together in a small bowl / Put the leaves into a bowl and toss in the dressing.

To serve

Cut wedges of tart and place on serving plates, with a pile of salad alongside.

Wine expert Olly Smith's choice
Sainsbury's Taste the Difference Austrian Grüner Veltliner

Michel Roux
Smoked haddock soufflé

You only need one soufflé recipe in your repetoire and this is it, from the Master. C'est parfait!

Ingredients Serves 4

Béchamel
30g (1¼oz) butter
30g (1¼oz) flour
400ml (14fl oz) milk

Soufflé
6 egg yolks
40g (1½oz) butter, softened
110g (4oz) Gruyère cheese, finely grated
125g (4½oz) smoked haddock fillet
300ml (11fl oz) double cream
8 egg whites (about 275ml/10fl oz)
1 tablespoon roughly chopped fresh dill

To serve
4 poached quail's eggs (optional)
4 sprigs of fresh dill

Method

Béchamel
Preheat the oven to 190°C/375F/Gas 5 / To make the béchamel, melt the butter in a small heavy-based saucepan / Off the heat, stir in the flour, then return the pan to a low heat and cook for 2 minutes, stirring continuously with a small whisk / Off the heat, pour in the milk, stirring, then place on a medium heat and bring to the boil, stirring all the time / Reduce the heat and simmer for about 5 minutes, still stirring continuously.

Soufflé
Off the heat, mix the 6 egg yolks into the hot béchamel and season with salt and black pepper / Cover this soufflé base with clingfilm and set aside at room temperature / With the butter, grease the insides of 4 individual soufflé dishes 10cm (4 inches) in diameter and 6.5cm (2¾ inches) deep / Sprinkle a handful of the grated Gruyère into one soufflé dish, rotate it to coat the inside, then tip the excess into a second dish / Repeat the process to coat all 4 dishes / Put the smoked haddock into a small saucepan, pour on the cream and place over a low heat / When the cream starts bubbling, reduce the heat to a gentle simmer and cook for 2 minutes / Turn off the heat and leave until cool enough to handle, then remove the fish skin and flake the flesh with your fingertips, removing any small bones and putting the fish back into the cream / In a clean bowl, beat the egg whites with a pinch of salt to soft peaks / Whisk one third of the egg whites into the soufflé base to loosen it, then add this mixture to the remaining egg whites and fold in delicately, using a spatula, adding the remaining Gruyère and the dill as you go / Half-fill each prepared dish with the soufflé mixture, then spoon in the creamy haddock mix / Fill the dishes with the remaining soufflé mixture to the top and smooth the surface with a palette knife / Run a knife around the edge of the mixture to ease it away from the side of the dish – this helps the soufflé to rise / Stand the soufflé dishes in a roasting tin and pour in enough boiling water to come halfway up the sides / Cook in the oven for 7 to 8 minutes.

To serve

Top each soufflé with a quail's egg, if you like, and a sprig of dill, and serve immediately.

Wine expert Peter Richards's choice
Bourgogne Chardonnay
You get a gorgeous persistence of flavour with this wine, but it's very soft and gentle. You get those wonderful nutty, creamy, buttery aromas that are the classic flavours of top white Burgundy.

Lawrence Keogh
Poached sea trout with vanilla salad cream, heritage tomatoes and samphire

Heritage tomatoes come in all sorts of varieties and colours – choose a mixture of colours for added impact.

Ingredients Serves 4

Trout
1 carrot, chopped
½ leek, chopped
1 onion, chopped
½ head of fennel, chopped
1 celery stick, chopped
¼ bunch of fresh thyme
2 bay leaves
¼ bunch fresh parsley stalks
8 white peppercorns
¼ teaspoon sea salt
Juice of 1 lemon
250ml (9fl oz) white wine vinegar
1 litre (1¾ pints) water
4 x 150g (5oz) sea trout fillet, skin on

Salad cream
50g (2oz) plain flour
20g (¾oz) English mustard powder
1 tablespoon olive oil
50g (2oz) caster sugar
1 egg
570ml (1 pint) milk
2 tablespoons white wine vinegar
1 vanilla pod, split and seeds scraped out
Juice of ½ lemon

Tomatoes and samphire
1kg (2lb 2oz) heritage tomatoes, thickly sliced
75ml (3fl oz) rapeseed oil
500g (1lb 2oz) samphire

Method

Trout
Place all the ingredients except the trout in a saucepan and bring to the boil / Turn the heat down slightly and simmer for 10 minutes – this gives you a court bouillon / Place the sea trout, skin side down, in a container deep enough to take all the court bouillon / Pour the hot court bouillon over and set aside until the liquid is cool.

Salad cream
Place the flour and mustard powder in a saucepan and mix together / Season, add the olive oil and sugar and mix together / Whisk the egg into the milk / Place the saucepan on the heat and heat gently / Add the milk mixture gradually, whisking all the time, until the mixture is simmering / Cook for a further 10–15 minutes, until thick and glossy, whisking occasionally / Add the vinegar and whisk once more / Remove from the heat and add the vanilla seeds and lemon juice / Whisk to combine and check the seasoning, then set aside to cool.

Tomatoes and samphire
Season the tomatoes with rapeseed oil and a little salt and black pepper / Bring a pan of salted water to the boil, add the samphire and cook for 1–2 minutes then drain and refresh in cold water.

To serve

Take the sea trout out of the court bouillon, remove the skin and scrape off any brown flesh / Place the slices of tomato in a stack on each serving plate, alternating the colours / Place a pile of samphire next to the tomatoes, and top with the sea trout / Spoon the vanilla salad cream to one side and finish with a drizzle of rapeseed oil.

Wine expert Olly Smith's choice
Sainsbury's Taste the Difference Chablis
Chablis should be all about zest, verve, brightness, all the twinkle of the stars. It's all about finesse, fine tuning and most crucially, freshness. It's the perfect wine for summer sipping.

Jun Tanaka
Red mullet with almonds, escabeche and butternut purée

This dish is spectacular and looks beautiful on the plate. It was a real showstopper in the studio.

Ingredients Serves 4

Escabeche
150ml (5fl oz) olive oil
200g (7oz) carrots, thinly sliced
110g (4oz) shallots, cut into rings
50g (2oz) baby fennel, sliced
1 garlic clove, crushed
1 teaspoon coriander seeds, crushed
1 sprig of fresh thyme
Pinch of saffron
75ml (3fl oz) white balsamic vinegar
50ml (2fl oz) water

Butternut purée
25g (1oz) butter
250g (9oz) butternut squash, peeled and cut into 2cm pieces
50ml (2fl oz) chicken stock
25ml (1fl oz) double cream

Red mullet
50g (2oz) flaked almonds, toasted
1 sprig of fresh rosemary, leaves stripped and chopped
1 egg white
4 red mullet fillets, skin and tail left on
50ml (2fl oz) olive oil
25g (1oz) butter

Method

Escabeche
Heat a shallow pan until just warm, then add the olive oil, carrots, shallots and fennel and cook on a gentle heat for 5 minutes / Season, add the garlic, coriander, thyme and saffron, and cook for a further 2 minutes / Pour in the vinegar, add the water and bring to a simmer / Cook for 5 minutes and remove from the heat – the vegetables should be slightly crunchy / Leave to cool, then place in the fridge, ideally overnight, to allow the flavours to infuse.

Butternut purée
Heat a frying pan, add the butter and butternut squash, and season with salt and black pepper / Cover and cook for 10 minutes / Pour in the stock, bring to a simmer and then cook for a further 10 minutes / Add the cream and boil for 1 minute / Place in a blender and blitz to a purée, then check the seasoning, set aside and keep warm while you cook the mullet.

Red mullet
Mix the almonds with the rosemary and place on a tray / Pour the egg white on to a separate tray / Dip the mullet, skin side down, into the egg white, then press on to the almonds / Pour the olive oil into a non-stick pan, season the fish, place in the pan almond side down and cook for 2 minutes / Add the butter, flip over the mullet and cook for a further 2 minutes.

To serve

Spoon the purée on to serving plates, place the escabeche alongside and finally add the red mullet on top.

Wine expert Olly Smith's choice
Saint-Romain Chardonnay
The oak in this wine makes it smell quite nutty and that's going to pick up brilliantly on the almonds in the dish. It just lasts so long in the mouth, which is a real indication of quality in a fine wine.

Rick Stein
Seared swordfish steaks with salmoriglio, tomato and pepper

Salmoriglio originates from Sicily and usually accompanies grilled meat or fish. This dish is equally great on the barbecue or on the griddle.

Ingredients Serves 4

Salad
2 red peppers
500g (1lb 2oz) tomatoes
1 small red onion, finely chopped
60g (2½oz) preserved lemon, flesh removed and discarded, skin chopped into small pieces
2 tablespoons chopped fresh coriander

Dressing
1½ tablespoons lemon juice
3 tablespoons extra virgin olive oil
1 medium-hot red chilli, deseeded and finely chopped
1 garlic clove, finely chopped

Swordfish
4 x 200–225g (7–8oz) swordfish steaks, about 2cm (¾ inch) thick
2 tablespoons olive oil
Peperoncino or crushed dried chillies

Salmoriglio
6 tablespoons extra virgin olive oil
3 tablespoons water
1½ tablespoons lemon juice
1 garlic clove, very finely chopped
1 tablespoon chopped fresh oregano
1 tablespoon chopped celery cress or celery tops
1 tablespoon chopped fresh flat-leaf parsley

Method

Salad
Preheat the oven to 220°C/425°F/Gas 7 / Roast the red peppers in the oven for 20 minutes, turning them once / Seal them in a plastic bag and leave to cool / Break the peppers open, discard the stalk, seeds and skin and cut the flesh into short chunky strips / Skin the tomatoes, halve them, remove the seeds and then cut them into small, chunky pieces / Set aside until required.

Dressing
Whisk the lemon juice and olive oil together and stir in the red chilli, garlic and some salt and black pepper to taste / Set aside until required.

Swordfish
If you are using a charcoal barbecue, light it 40 minutes before you want to start cooking / If you are using a gas barbecue, light it 10 minutes beforehand / If you are using a ridged cast-iron griddle, leave it over a high heat for a couple of minutes until smoking hot, then reduce the heat to medium high / Brush the swordfish generously with olive oil and season well with salt, peperoncino or crushed dried chillies and black pepper / Cook over a medium high heat for 4 minutes on each side.

Salmoriglio
Shortly before cooking the swordfish, make the salmoriglio / Whisk the olive oil and water together in a bowl until thick and creamy and then whisk in the lemon juice and some salt to taste / Stir in the garlic, oregano, celery cress or tops and parsley.

To serve

Place the swordfish on serving plates and drizzle over the salmoriglio / Place the tomatoes next to the swordfish and top with the peppers, followed by the red onion and preserved lemon / Drizzle the dressing over the salad and sprinkle over the chopped coriander.

Wine expert Olly Smith's choice
Montes Limited Selection Sauvignon Blanc
This is invigoration in a bottle. It's got the zip to cut through the meaty texture of the swordfish and the crispness to really make the salmoriglio sing!

Matthew Fort
Sgombro alla griglia con capperi e bobbia

Matthew's better known for his critiquing skills than his cooking but he gave us a chance to see how good his own food is with this lovely Sicilian dish.

Ingredients Serves 4

Mackerel
4 small mackerel
4 very ripe tomatoes, deseeded and chopped
50g (2oz) capers in salt, rinsed and drained
Juice of 1 lemon

Potatoes
3 tablespoons olive oil
500g (1lb 2oz) waxy potatoes, peeled and cut into 3cm (1¼ inch) cubes
1 red pepper, thinly sliced
1 yellow pepper, thinly sliced
2 garlic cloves, finely sliced
25ml (1fl oz) white wine

Method

Mackerel
Preheat the grill to high / Slash the sides of the mackerel and season with salt and black pepper / Place on a grill tray and grill for 3-4 minutes on each side / Place the mackerel in a deep serving dish / Plaster them with the chopped tomatoes / Scatter the capers all over / Pour the mackerel juices over and sprinkle the lemon juice over everything.

Potatoes
Heat a frying pan until just warm, add the oil, potatoes, peppers and garlic and mix around / Add the white wine and cook gently, stirring from time to time to prevent sticking, until the potatoes are cooked through and the peppers are soft / Season with salt and black pepper and serve the mackerel and potatoes together.

Wine expert Olly Smith's choice
Lawson's Dry Hills Marlborough Sauvignon Blanc
A pungent wine will work best here, complementing the punchy flavours of the capers and garlic. This Sauvignon Blanc from New Zealand also has a crispness that will cut through the texture of the oily fish.

Atul Kochhar
Vava meen roast
(South Indian fish sandwich)

We suggest you eat this sandwich with a knife and fork, not your fingers! A beautifully elegant, delicately spiced dish.

Ingredients Serves 4

Crab mixture
5–6 tablespoons vegetable oil
1 teaspoon cumin seeds
2 green cardamom pods
1 bay leaf
2.5cm (1 inch) piece of
   cinnamon stick
3 cloves
5 black peppercorns
2 onions, chopped
25g (1oz) ginger and garlic
   paste or equal quantities
   of ginger and garlic pastes
   mixed with a little water
3 tomatoes, chopped
¼ teaspoon turmeric
1½ teaspoons ground
   coriander
½ teaspoon red chilli powder
250g (9oz) fresh white
   crabmeat
1 tablespoon finely chopped
   fresh coriander leaves

Plaice
½ teaspoon red chilli powder
1 teaspoon ground coriander
½ teaspoon ground turmeric
2 tablespoons tamarind pulp
4 small plaice, filleted

To serve
16 cherry tomatoes, halved
1 punnet of cress
1 teaspoon balsamic vinegar
1 tablespoon extra virgin
   olive oil
¼ teaspoon turmeric

Method

Crab mixture

Heat the vegetable oil in a sauté pan, add the cumin, cardamom, bay leaf, cinnamon, cloves and peppercorns and sauté until they crackle / Add the onions and sauté until light brown, then stir in the ginger–garlic paste and sauté for 2–3 minutes / Add the tomatoes, turmeric, coriander and chilli powder and sauté for 8–10 minutes, until the tomatoes have turned into a thick sauce / Stir in the crabmeat, season with salt if necessary, then sprinkle with the chopped coriander and set aside while you prepare the plaice.

Plaice

Preheat the grill / Mix together the chilli powder, coriander, turmeric, tamarind and some salt and spread over the flesh side of the plaice fillets / Set aside to marinate for about 10 minutes / When ready to cook the plaice, put the fillets on a baking tray, place under the hot grill, flesh side up, and cook for 1–2 minutes, until the flesh firms up a little / Sandwich the fillets together with the crab mixture, making sure the skin is on the outside / Return to the grill for 3–5 minutes, turning once, until the fish is completely cooked.

To serve

Place a fish sandwich in the centre of each serving plate / Pile the tomatoes alongside and top with some cress / Whisk the vinegar, oil and turmeric together and drizzle around the fish.

Wine expert Peter Richards's choice
Shepherds Ridge Sauvignon Blanc Marlborough
For this dish you need a wine that's going to stand up to all the flavours, but you don't want something too big that's going to clash. There are loads of lovely clean, fresh, pure aromatics in this wine.

Vivek Singh
Grilled mackerel fillets with cloves, fennel, pepper and cinnamon, yoghurt kadhi and curry leaf spinach poriyal

This recipe turns the cheap and humble mackerel into a superstar dinner party dish.

Ingredients Serves 4

Yoghurt kadhi
175g (6oz) yoghurt
1 tablespoon gram flour
250ml (9fl oz) water
½ teaspoon salt
¼ teaspoon turmeric
1 tablespoon ghee
1 whole red chilli
½ teaspoon cumin seeds
1 sprig of curry leaves
Juice of ½ lemon

Mackerel
1 teaspoon cloves
1 teaspoon fennel seeds
½ teaspoon black
    peppercorns
5cm (2 inch) piece of
    cinnamon stick
1 teaspoon cumin seeds
½ teaspoon red chilli powder
1 teaspoon salt
4 large mackerel fillets, skin
    on, pin-boned and trimmed
1 tablespoon vegetable oil
Juice of ½ lemon

Spinach poriyal
2 tablespoons oil
1 teaspoon mustard seeds
1 sprig of curry leaves
1 onion, finely chopped
½ teaspoon salt
1 fresh green chilli, deseeded
    and finely chopped
150g (5oz) spinach stalks and
    leaves, finely shredded
60g (2½oz) fresh coconut,
    grated

Method

Yoghurt kadhi
Whisk together the yoghurt, gram flour, water, salt and turmeric and pass through a seive to lose any lumps / Place in a pan over a medium heat and bring to the boil, whisking continuously – the flour will catch if left without stirring / When it comes to the boil, reduce the heat and let it simmer for 5–8 minutes, until the sauce turns glossy and begins to coat the back of a wooden spoon / Skim to get rid of any scum or impurities / In a metal ladle held directly over the heat, heat the ghee and bring to smoking point / Add the red chilli, cumin and curry leaves and allow to splutter and crackle for 3–6 seconds, then tip the contents of the ladle over the sauce and set aside.

Mackerel
Preheat the grill / Pound together all the spices and the salt to a coarse consistency and sprinkle over the fish on both sides / Mix the oil and lemon juice and drizzle over the fish / Place the fish on a grill tray, skin side up, and cook for 8–10 minutes, or until the fillets are just cooked.

Spinach poriyal
While the fish is cooking, heat some oil in a frying pan, add the mustard seeds and curry leaves and allow to crackle for 10–15 seconds / Add the onion and cook for about 5–6 minutes, until translucent / Now add the salt and chilli and stir for a minute / Add the spinach and cook for 2–3 minutes, stirring so that it cooks evenly / Finally add the coconut and stir well to heat through.

To serve

Pour the yoghurt kadhi into deep serving bowls or plates and sit the fish on top, then place the spinach poriyal over the fish.

Wine expert Peter Richards's choice
Torres Viña Esmeralda
We need something with loads of aromatic power to stand up to the pungent spices, and something that's soft and rich to match the spicy heat from the chilli. This rare blend of Muscat and Gewürztraminer is the best option.

Patrick Williams
Roast red bream with fried plantain fritters and coconut sauce

This is a great example of modern Caribbean food. Green plantain are savoury, but as they ripen to yellow they sweeten so make sure you buy green for this recipe.

Ingredients Serves 4

Sauce
2 tablespoons olive oil
1 onion, finely diced
1 garlic clove, crushed
1 red pepper, finely diced
1 teaspoon curry powder
Water from 2 coconuts
2 tomatoes, blanched, deseeded and finely diced
50g (2oz) butter

Fritters
2 green plantain, grated
75g (3oz) self-raising flour
1 egg
75ml (3fl oz) Red Stripe lager
1 tablespoon roughly chopped fresh coriander

Bream
4 red bream fillets, skin on
1 teaspoon freshly ground pimento seeds
1 garlic clove, sliced
2 sprigs of fresh thyme
4 tablespoons olive oil

Spinach
1 tablespoon olive oil
150g (5oz) baby leaf spinach
Pinch of nutmeg

To serve
1 punnet of shiso

Method

Sauce
Heat a frying pan, add the olive oil, the onion and garlic and cook for 20 seconds without colouring / Add the red pepper and curry powder and cook for 1 minute / Add the coconut water and bring to the boil, then reduce the heat and cook until the liquid has reduced by half / Add the tomatoes and butter to the pan and cook until emulsified / Check the seasoning and set aside to keep warm.

Fritters
Heat a deep-fat fryer to 180°C / Place the grated plantain into a bowl / Place the flour and egg into a second bowl / Whisk the lager into the flour and egg to form a thick batter / Season with salt and black pepper and add the coriander / Pour the batter over the plantain and mix so all the plantain is coated / Drop spoonfuls of the battered plantain into the hot oil for 2–3 minutes or until golden brown / Drain on kitchen paper.

Bream
While the oil for the fritters is heating up, place the fish on a plate / Place the ground pimento, garlic and thyme in a bowl and mix with 3 tablespoons of the olive oil / Pour over the fish and toss to coat, then set aside for at least 5 minutes / When the fritters are cooked, heat a frying pan, add the remaining tablespoon of olive oil and the fish, skin side down, and fry for 2 minutes on each side.

Spinach
Meanwhile heat a sauté pan, add the oil and the spinach and cook until just wilted / Season with salt, black pepper and nutmeg.

To serve
Place some spinach in the centre of each serving plate / Top with the red bream, and place 5 fritters around the plate / Spoon the sauce over the fish, finishing with a few shiso leaves.

Wine expert Olly Smith's choice
Charles Back Chenin Blanc/Viognier
This dish amplifies the aromatic qualities of ingredients like the cracked pimento and the coriander, so we need a wine with an extra dimension. With a splash of Viognier, this is a unique blend that's perfect.

John Torode
Brill en papillote

The whole team have tried this at home! It's such a simple dish, but it's a surefire hit. You have to try it too.

Ingredients Serves 4

Dressing
50ml (2fl oz) soy sauce
50ml (2fl oz) sake
50ml (2fl oz) mirin
1 tablespoon sesame oil

Brill
4 large pieces of banana leaves, steamed and softened, the hard edge removed so they roll up
2 carrots, cut into fine strips
3 spring onions, cut into fine strips
Small handful of fresh basil leaves
2 sprigs of fresh thyme, leaves picked
5cm piece of fresh root ginger, cut into fine strips
4 chunks of brill with the bone in, or 2 whole brill, skinned and boned

Method

Dressing
Whisk together the dressing ingredients in a bowl and set aside.

Brill
Preheat the oven to 230°C/450°F/Gas 8 / Place each banana leaf in a bowl and press down so that it follows the shape / Place some of the vegetables, herbs and ginger in the dip, and top with a piece of fish / Spoon a little of the dressing over the top / Top with some more vegetables and the rest of the dressing / Remove from the bowl, fold the leaf over the filling and tie with string so that it is sealed fully / Place on a baking tray in the oven and cook for 10–12 minutes / Alternatively, place on a barbecue and cook until it starts to bubble, then remove and leave to stand for 3 minutes.

To serve

Open up the leaves and serve with a big bowl of green salad.

Nic Watt
Sea bream marinated in ryotei miso with pickled onion salsa

The onion salsa keeps for a while in the fridge and would go really well with most things, including a big slab of Cheddar!

Ingredients Serves 4

Sea bream

500g (1lb 2oz) saikyo miso (sweet white miso)
2½ tablespoons caster sugar
3 tablespoons sake
3 tablespoons mirin
1 tablespoon light soy sauce
4 large sea bream fillets, skin on
4 tablespoons vegetable oil
1 lemon, cut into 4

Salsa

6 green beans, cut in half
200ml (7fl oz) rice wine vinegar
2 tablespoons caster sugar
1 small green chilli, deseeded and finely sliced
2 large red onions, finely sliced
2 red baby plum tomatoes, cut into quarters
2 yellow teardrop tomatoes, cut into quarters
½ punnet of rock chives

Method

Sea bream

Place the miso, sugar, sake, mirin and soy sauce in a bowl and whisk together / Coat the sea bream fillets in the vegetable oil, then cover generously with the miso paste / Place in the fridge and marinate for 2 hours / When ready to cook the fish, remove it from the marinade and place it skin side up on a board / Preheat the grill / Thread a metal skewer through the fish, starting 4cm (1½ inches) from the right-hand side of the tail end, working up diagonally towards the top of the fillet, waving the fish to form ripples / Repeat with a second skewer from the left-hand side / Place wedges of lemon on each end of the skewers and squeeze together to form big ripples / Place the skewered fish under the grill, skin side up, for 4 minutes, until golden / Turn and grill for 4 minutes on the flesh side, until golden brown and caramelised.

Salsa

Towards the end of the fish marinating time, bring a pan of salted water to the boil and add the green beans / Cook for 30 seconds, then drain the beans and plunge them into ice-cold water to stop the cooking process / Place the rice wine vinegar and caster sugar into a saucepan and bring to the boil / Place the chilli and onion slices in a bowl and pour over the hot vinegar / Cover and set aside for 30 minutes, until pickled / Toss together the tomatoes, beans, red onion pickle, rock chives and 1 teaspoon of the pickling vinegar together in a bowl, and add a little salt and black pepper.

To serve

Remove the lemons from the skewer, slide the fish on to plates and serve with a spoonful of the salsa alongside.

Wine expert Susie Barrie's choice
Arrowfield Estate Riesling
Australian or New World Rieslings tend to be drier and a bit more full-bodied. This one is as fresh and vibrant as the dish, but also has an exotic note to go with the heat.

Paul Rankin
Sesame-fried brill with soy mustard vinaigrette, Asian coleslaw and wontons

Paul was an innovator of Pacific Rim food, and this dish has a refreshing Asian twist on classic coleslaw.

Ingredients Serves 4

Coleslaw
⅛ white cabbage, finely shredded
1 small carrot, finely grated
2 tablespoons pickled ginger, finely chopped
3–4 tablespoons soy sauce, preferably Japanese
1 tablespoon caster sugar
½ tablespoon rice wine vinegar
2 tablespoons lime juice
1 tablespoon peanut butter
½ teaspoon chilli powder

Dressing
2 tablespoons wholegrain mustard
1 teaspoon English mustard
2 tablespoons caster sugar
2 tablespoons rice wine vinegar
2 tablespoons soy sauce, preferably Japanese
5 tablespoons vegetable oil

Wontons
1 packet of wonton skins or spring roll wrappers

Brill
4 x 150g (5oz) thick brill fillets, skinned
1 tablespoon white sesame seeds
1 tablespoon black sesame seeds
1 tablespoon vegetable oil
25g (1oz) butter

To serve
4 tablespoons chopped fresh coriander
2 tablespoons finely sliced spring onions
Chopped fresh chives, to garnish

Method

Coleslaw
In a ceramic or stainless steel bowl, combine all the ingredients / Allow to marinate for at least 1 hour (and up to 2–3 hours).

Dressing
Place both mustards, the sugar, vinegar and soy sauce in a bowl and whisk together until the sugar is dissolved / Gradually whisk in the oil until emulsified.

Wontons
When the coleslaw is ready, heat a deep-fat fryer to 180°C / Separate the wonton or spring roll wrappers, and cut into fine strips / Fry until crisp and golden brown then drain on kitchen paper, and season generously with salt.

Brill
Meanwhile, season the brill fillets with salt and black pepper and sprinkle the skinless side with the sesame seeds, pressing them firmly into the fish / Heat a large frying pan over a moderately high heat, add the oil and butter and, when the butter is foaming, put in the fish fillets, sesame seed side down / Fry for about 5 minutes, then turn carefully and cook for a further 3 minutes.

To serve

Lightly strain the excess liquid off the coleslaw and stir in the coriander and spring onions / Place the brill on serving plates and scatter with the chives / Spoon the coleslaw alongside, and top with the crispy wontons / Spoon the dressing around and over the fish.

Wine expert Peter Richards's choice
La Différence Viognier-Muscat
I've chosen something that's going to add to the dish, almost acting as a fruity counterpoint to all those lovely, spicy flavours. The Viognier adds sort of floral white peppery aromatics and the Muscat gives loads of sweet ripe fruit.

Michael Caines
Pan-fried grey mullet with a stir-fry of mangetout, shiitake mushrooms and lemongrass sauce

Grey mullet is inexpensive and often overlooked, but it tastes delicious. If you haven't tried it before, this recipe is a great introduction to the fish.

Ingredients Serves 4

Sauce
50g (2oz) butter
50g (2oz) shallots, sliced
75g (3oz) lemongrass
175g (6oz) button mushrooms, sliced
8g (⅓oz) finely chopped fresh lemon thyme
50ml (2fl oz) fish stock
250ml (9fl oz) Gewürztraminer/ Chardonnay wine
250ml (9fl oz) cream

Mullet
4 x 175g (6oz) grey mullet fillets, skin on scored
1 tablespoon olive oil
Juice of 1 lime

Vegetables
2 tablespoons sesame seed oil
60g (2½oz) beansprouts
60g (2½oz) shiitake mushrooms, cut in to julienne strips
60g (2½oz) mangetout, cut in to julienne strips
2 tablespoons toasted sesame seeds

Method

Sauce
Heat a frying pan and add half the butter, the shallots, lemongrass and a pinch of salt / Cook until the shallots are soft and translucent, about 4–5 minutes / Add the mushrooms and lemon thyme, and cook until the mushrooms look slightly wet / Add the fish stock and cook until the liquid is reduced by half / In a separate pan, boil the wine until it is reduced by a third, then add to the reduced stock / Add the cream, bring to the boil, cook until thickened slightly, then pass through a sieve into a clean pan / Whisk in the remaining half of butter, season with salt and black pepper, and set aside.

Mullet
Season the flesh side of the grey mullet with salt and black pepper / Heat a frying pan, add the olive oil and put in the fish, skin side down / When the skin of the mullet is golden brown and crispy, turn the fish over to finish cooking and drizzle with the lime juice.

Vegetables
Meanwhile heat the sesame seed oil in a second pan and stir-fry the beansprouts, shiitake mushrooms and mangetout with a pinch of salt / Once these have softened, add the toasted sesame seeds and stir.

To serve
Pile the vegetables on to serving plates / Place the fish on top of the vegetables and spoon over the sauce.

Wine expert Peter Richards's choice
Viña Real Rioja Blanco CVNE
White Rioja is often fermented in oak barrels, and what that means is you get lots of lovely buttery, nutty flavours, which are going to pick up really well on the cream and the sesame in this dish.

James Martin
Halibut with lychee, cashew nut and miso salad

If you've only tasted miso in soup, you'll be forgiven for thinking it's bland. This is a much more interesting way to use it and shows its versatility.

Ingredients Serves 4

Halibut
75ml (3fl oz) sake
75ml (3fl oz) mirin
225g (8oz) white miso paste
110g (4oz) granulated sugar
4 x 175g (6oz) halibut fillets, skin on

Salad
110g (4oz) fresh lychees, peeled, stoned and sliced
75g (3oz) toasted cashew nuts
1 small bunch of fresh mint, leaves picked
110g (4oz) mango, sliced
1 small bunch of fresh coriander, leaves picked
1 red chilli, deseeded and finely sliced on the diagonal
50g (2oz) coconut shavings
110g (4oz) mizuna leaves
50g (2oz) rocket leaves
Juice of 1 lime
2 tablespoons groundnut oil

Method

Halibut
Place the sake and mirin in a saucepan and bring to the boil / Boil for 20–30 seconds to burn off the alcohol, then reduce the heat / Add the white miso and stir to dissolve / Turn the heat back up and add the sugar, stirring once more to dissolve / Remove from the heat, transfer to a glass bowl and leave to cool / Set one-third of the miso mixture aside for the salad / Place the halibut fillets in the remaining cold miso mixture, then cover and place in the fridge for at least 24 hours, preferably 48 hours / When you are ready to cook the fish, preheat the grill to high and the oven to 200°C/400°F/Gas 6 / Remove the halibut from the miso and wipe off any excess, then place on a grill tray / Place under the grill for 2–3 minutes, until golden, then transfer to the oven for 5–8 minutes.

Salad
While the halibut is in the oven, place all the salad ingredients except the lime juice and groundnut oil in a bowl and toss together / Take 2 tablespoons of the reserved miso mixture, add the lime juice and groundnut oil, whisk to combine, and season with salt and black pepper / Toss some of the dressing with the salad.

To serve
Spoon the salad into the centre of your serving plates / Place the halibut on top of the salad and drizzle over a little more miso dressing.

Wine expert Peter Richards's choice
Cono Sur Gewürztraminer, Bio Bio Valley

Nic Watt
Crispy lemon sole with chilli, sesame and soy

This is just eye-poppingly spectacular – it tastes as good as it looks, and yes, you really can eat the whole thing.

Ingredients Serves 2

Marinade and dipping sauce
1 teaspoon chopped green chilli
1 teaspoon chopped red chilli
1 teaspoon chopped fresh root ginger
½ teaspoon chopped garlic
2 teaspoons ground coriander
1 teaspoon black sesame seeds
1 teaspoon Dijon mustard
1 teaspoon sesame oil
50ml (2fl oz) soy sauce
Juice of ½ lemon
5 tablespoons vegetable oil

Sole
2 lemon sole
50–75g (2–3oz) potato starch

To serve
Zest of 2 lemons
2 teaspoons Yukari seasoning
2 green chillies, sliced into rings
4 sprigs of fresh coriander, leaves picked

Method

Marinade and dipping sauce
Place all the ingredients except the vegetable oil into a bowl and whisk to combine / Heat the vegetable oil on a high heat until it reaches smoking point / Pour the hot oil into the bowl and stir – the sauce should splatter a little when the oil is added / Divide the sauce between 2 bowls – half for the marinade and half for the dipping sauce.

Sole
Heat a deep-fat fryer to 190°C / Scale, clean and fillet the fish / Clean the skeletons, then cut in half lengthways, keeping the backbone intact on one half / Discard the halves without the backbone / Skin the sole fillets and cut each fillet into bite-size pieces / Put the sole into one of the sauce bowls and leave to marinate for 15 minutes / Meanwhile, dust the sole skeletons with some of the potato starch / As best you can, one at a time, press the sole skeletons around a metal bowl and hold in place with a metal ladle, then carefully place everything in the hot oil to cook for 2–3 minutes / As they cook, the skeletons will harden into the bowl shape – this will become an edible serving dish / Drain on kitchen paper / Lift the sole from the marinade and coat evenly in the remaining potato starch / Shake to remove any excess flour, then drop into the fat fryer and fry for 2–3 minutes, until lightly golden / Drain on kitchen paper.

To serve
Place the curved sole skeletons on your serving plates and arrange the fish pieces on them / Sprinkle generously with the fresh lemon zest, yukari seasoning, chilli slices and coriander leaves / Serve with a little bowl of dipping sauce.

Wine expert Tim Atkin's choice
Villa Maria Gewürztraminer Private Bin
This is a brilliant wine match for all sorts of oriental food. There's a lovely touch of ginger, and enough sweetness in it to take the sting out of the chilli but also compliment the saltiness of the soy sauce.

Rick Stein
Fish tacos from Baja California with guacamole

This is one of Rick's classics, and it will become one of your favourites too. It's really accessible and tasty, and the simple guacamole is delicious.

Ingredients Serves 4

Salsa

1 red onion, finely chopped
5 tomatoes, peeled, deseeded and finely chopped
3–4 medium-hot chillies, deseeded and finely chopped
1 teaspoon sugar
Juice of 1 lime
4 tablespoons roughly chopped fresh coriander

Guacamole

1 large avocado, peeled and stoned
1 green chilli, deseeded
Juice of 1 lime
2 spring onions, chopped
1 tablespoon roughly chopped fresh coriander
3 tablespoons vegetable oil
½ teaspoon salt

Tacos

2 sea bass, about 350g (12oz) each, filleted
225g (8oz) plain flour
2 eggs
200ml (7fl oz) water
8 soft flour tortillas

To serve

225g (8oz) iceberg lettuce, finely shredded
300ml (10oz) soured cream

Method

Salsa

Place all the ingredients in a bowl with a pinch of salt and mix well.

Guacamole

Place all the ingredients into a food processor and blend until smooth.

Tacos

Heat a deep-fat fryer to 190°C / Cut the fish fillets across into strips 1cm (½ inch) wide and season with plenty of salt and black pepper / Place the flour, eggs, water and a pinch of salt into a liquidiser and blend until smooth / Warm the tortillas in a low oven or a microwave / Dip the strips of fish into the batter, then drop them into the hot oil and fry for 4 minutes, until crisp and golden / Lift out with a slotted spoon and drain briefly on kitchen paper.

To serve

Place some lettuce down the centre of each tortilla, top with fried fish, then spoon over some salsa and soured cream / Fold in the sides, roll up as tightly as you can and serve straight away with a dollop of guacamole.

Wine expert Peter Richards's choice
Castillo de Molina Sauvignon Blanc Reserva
This is a delicious match, full of vibrant, lemony acidity that is going to work really well with the sea bass but also pick up nicely on the lime and tomato in the salsa.

Ken Hom
Stir-fried salmon with lemon and basmati rice

The salmon may tend to flake at the edges as it cooks, but don't worry if this happens, it will still taste great.

Ingredients Serves 4

Rice
400g (14oz) basmati rice
600ml (1 pint) water

Salmon
450g (1lb) boneless salmon
  fillet
2 teaspoons salt
4 tablespoons groundnut oil
1 tablespoon finely shredded
  fresh root ginger
1 teaspoon sugar
1 tablespoon lemon zest
1 lemon, segmented
2 teaspoons sesame oil

Method

Rice
Ideally the rice should be sufficient to fill a measuring jug to 400ml (14 fl oz) level / Put the rice into a large bowl and wash it in several changes of water until the water becomes clear / Drain the rice, put it into a heavy-based pan with the water and bring it to the boil / Continue boiling until most of the surface liquid has evaporated – this should take about 15 minutes, and the surface of the rice should have small indentations like a pitted crater / At this point, cover the pan with a very tight-fitting lid, turn the heat as low as possible and let the rice cook undisturbed for 15 minutes / There is no need to 'fluff' the rice, just let it rest for 5 minutes before serving it.

Salmon
When you start cooking the rice, cut the salmon into strips 2.5cm (1 inch) wide and sprinkle the salt evenly over them / Set aside for 20 minutes / When the rice is cooked and resting, heat a wok or large frying pan over a high heat, add 3 tablespoons of the groundnut oil, and when it is very hot and slightly smoking, turn the heat down to medium and add the salmon strips / Let them fry undisturbed for about 2 minutes, then gently turn them over until they are brown on both sides, taking care not to break them up / Remove them from the pan with a slotted spoon and drain on kitchen paper / Wipe the wok clean, reheat it, add the remaining tablespoon of groundnut oil and the ginger, and stir-fry for 20 seconds / Now add the sugar, lemon zest, lemon segments, some salt and black pepper and stir-fry gently for about 1 minute / Return the salmon to the wok and gently mix with the lemon for about 1 minute / Add the sesame oil and give the mixture a good stir.

To serve

Using a slotted spoon, arrange the salmon and lemon on a warm serving platter and serve with the rice.

Wine expert Peter Richards's choice
The Reach Sauvignon Blanc
This wine has got a lovely aromatic character that goes really well with Asian cuisine. Like any good Kiwi Sauvignon Blanc, it just leaps out of the glass at you.

Jason Atherton
Tuna with a soy, ginger and chilli glaze with bok choi

Jason loves cooking simple, Asian dishes like this one at home for his family.

Ingredients Serves 4

Shallots
2 small shallots, finely sliced into rings
4–6 tablespoons olive oil

Tuna
4 x 350g (12oz) tuna fillets
2 tablespoons sunflower oil
6 tablespoons dark soy sauce
4 tablespoons balsamic vinegar
1 garlic clove, finely chopped
2.5cm (1 inch) piece of fresh root ginger, very finely chopped
1 medium hot red chilli, deseeded and finely chopped

Bok choi
450g (1lb) small heads of bok choi, halved lengthways
½ teaspoon roasted sesame oil
2.5cm (1 inch) piece of fresh root ginger, finely shredded
¼ teaspoon salt
1 teaspoon cornflour
1 teaspoon water

To serve
4 sprigs of fresh coriander, to garnish

Method

Shallots
Wash the shallots in cold water then drain well and pat dry / Heat the oil in a frying pan, drop in the shallots and fry until golden / Drain on kitchen paper and set aside.

Tuna
Season the tuna fillets lightly on both sides with salt and black pepper / Heat the oil in a large pan over a high heat, then add the tuna fillets and sear them for 30 seconds on each side / Take the pan off the heat and add all the remaining ingredients / Reduce the heat to medium, return the pan to the heat and cook for 3 minutes, until the tuna is just cooked through.

Bok choi
Meanwhile bring a large pan of salted water to the boil, add the bok choi and cook for 3 minutes / Remove the bok choi and place on a plate to keep warm / Pour 150ml (5fl oz) of the cooking water into a small pan / Add the sesame oil, shredded ginger and salt to the reserved bok choi cooking liquor and bring to the boil / Whisk the cornflour and water together, then whisk into the liquid and simmer for 1 minute until thickened.

To serve

Divide the bok choi between your serving plates and spoon over some of the sesame and ginger flavoured sauce / Cut the tuna in half and lay on top of the bok choi / Garnish with the coriander sprigs and crispy shallots.

Wine expert Olly Smith's choice
Crios Torrontes
This one's got an almost lime marmalade tang to it and a surprising amount of texture, and that's going to work brilliantly with the meaty nature of the tuna.

James Martin
Roasted dover sole with caper butter and sautéd broad beans and potatoes

This simple spring recipe is one of James's absolute favourites; he'd have it every day if he could!

Ingredients Serves 4

Butter
150g (5oz) butter, melted
Zest of 1 lemon
2 tablespoons roughly chopped fresh flat-leaf parsley
2 tablespoons roughly chopped dill
1 banana shallot, roughly chopped
3 tablespoons capers, drained

Sole
4 whole Dover sole, skinned

Beans and potatoes
50g (2oz) butter
150g (5oz) broad beans, blanched and podded
2 tablespoons roughly chopped mint
200g (7oz) potatoes, cooked and sliced
1 garlic clove, roughly chopped
2 tablespoons roughly chopped fresh flat-leaf parsley

Method

Butter
Place all the ingredients except the capers into a food processor and blitz to a smooth paste / Add the capers and mix well / Spoon on to a piece of clingfilm and form into a roll, twisting the ends / Place in the fridge until required.

Sole
Preheat the oven to 190°C/375°F/Gas 5 and get an ovenproof griddle pan very hot / Season the fish with salt and black pepper and place on the griddle pan for 1 minute, until just marked / Remove the fish from the pan, turn it 90 degrees, and place it back on the griddle pan / Cook for a further minute, then place the whole griddle pan in the oven for 8–10 minutes, until the fish is cooked through.

Beans and potatoes
While the fish is in the oven, heat a frying pan, add half the butter and the broad beans and sauté for 2 minutes / Add the mint and season with black pepper / Heat a second frying pan and add the remaining butter and the potatoes / Sauté for 2–3 minutes, then add the garlic and sauté for a further minute / Add the parsley and season with salt and black pepper.

To serve

Place the fish on a heatproof serving plate and top with several slices of the caper butter / Place under a hot grill to just melt the butter / Spoon the potatoes and broad beans alongside the fish.

Wine expert Tim Atkin's choice
Sainsbury's Taste the Difference Grüner Veltliner

James Tanner
Pan-fried fillet of sea bass, sautéd baby gem with prawn and chorizo cassoulet

The cassoulet is really delicious and would work as a meal on its own.

Ingredients Serves 2

Cassoulet

300g (11oz) dried haricots blancs
1.5 litres (2½ pints) fish stock
2 sprigs of fresh thyme
2 bay leaves
300g (11oz) raw tiger prawns, shell on
1 tablespoon olive oil
1 garlic clove, roughly chopped
1 banana shallot, roughly chopped
1 leek, white only, roughly chopped
2 teaspoons tomato purée
¼ teaspoon cayenne pepper
75ml (3fl oz) dry vermouth or Noilly Prat
110ml (4fl oz) whipping cream
150g (5oz) semi-cured chorizo, roughly chopped
2 spring onions, finely sliced
40g (1½oz) butter
Juice of 1 lemon
6 sprigs of fresh chervil, roughly chopped

Sea bass

1 x 450g (1lb) wild sea bass, scaled, filleted and pin-boned
1 tablespoon olive oil
1 baby gem lettuce, leaves separated

To serve

4 sprigs of fresh chervil

Method

Cassoulet

Place the haricots blancs in a stainless steel container and cover with water / Leave overnight to soak, then drain and rinse / Place in a saucepan and cover with half the fish stock / Add the thyme and bay and bring to a boil / Reduce the heat and simmer for 30 minutes until just soft, then drain and set the beans aside / Shell half the prawns, keeping the shells, and reserving the shelled prawns for later / Roughly chop the remaining whole prawns and add to the shells / Heat a sauté pan, add the olive oil, garlic, shallot and leek and sauté for 1 minute / Add the chopped prawns and shells and cook for a further minute / Add the tomato purée and cayenne pepper and cook for another minute / Add the vermouth and flame to burn off the alcohol / Pour over the remaining stock and bring to the boil / Simmer for 5–8 minutes, then add the cream / Place in a blender and blitz to a purée, then pass through a fine sieve into a saucepan / Heat a frying pan, add the chorizo and cook for a minute / Add the cooked beans, raw prawns and spring onions and sauté for 2 minutes / Add a little of the sauce to the pan to just coat, and simmer until the prawns have just cooked through / Stir in with the butter, lemon juice and chervil and season with salt and black pepper.

Sea bass

Place the sea bass on a board and score the skin at 1cm (½ inch) intervals / Heat a frying pan, add the olive oil and place the sea bass in, skin side down / Cook for 2 minutes, then flip over and cook for a further 2 minutes / Add the little gem leaves to the fish and wilt slightly / Remove from the pan and drain on kitchen paper.

To serve

Pile the cassoulet into a bowl and top with the wilted baby gems / Place the fish on top and spoon the reserved sauce around / Garnish with the chervil sprigs.

Wine expert Peter Richards's choice
Gnarly Petit Verdot/Shiraz Rosé
This rosé combines the best of white and red wine. It's got that lovely freshness and delicacy of a white but the juiciness, body and spice of a red.

Marcus Wareing
Sea trout with liquorice carrots, sautéd baby gem and bisque

When Marcus suggested this dish we were intrigued by the combination, but the carrots and liquorice work brilliantly together.

Ingredients Serves 4

Bisque
40g (1½oz) butter
300g (11oz) langoustine heads
2 large carrots, roughly chopped
½ onion, roughly chopped
½ stick celery, roughly chopped
½ bunch of fresh thyme
½ bunch of fresh tarragon
6 star anise
75ml (3fl oz) brandy
50ml (2fl oz) Pernod
1 litre (1¾ pints) chicken stock
110ml (4fl oz) double cream

Trout
50g (2oz) butter
4 x 175g (6oz) sea trout fillets
2 tablespoons cumin seeds, toasted
½ bunch of fresh chervil, chopped

Carrots
60g (2½oz) butter
2 large carrots, cut into 3mm (⅛ inch) dice
110ml (4fl oz) chicken stock
2 liquorice logs, cut into 3mm (⅛ inch) dice (look for the softer, natural variety)
2 tablespoons olive oil
2 baby gem lettuces, leaves separated

Method

Bisque
Preheat the oven to 200°C/400°F/Gas 6 / Heat an ovenproof frying pan, add the butter and langoustine heads and fry for 2–3 minutes / Place in the oven for 10 minutes, then remove and place on the heat / Add the vegetables, herbs and star anise and sauté for 3–4 minutes / Add the brandy and Pernod and flame to burn off the alcohol / Cook for 1 minute, then add the stock / Bring to the boil and cook for a further 30 minutes, then strain, season and stir in the cream.

Trout
Heat a frying pan and add the butter / Add the trout and fry on each side for 2 minutes / Remove from the pan and sprinkle with the cumin seeds and chervil / Rest for 2–3 minutes before serving.

Carrots
Heat a saucepan and then add the butter and carrots / Add the stock and bring to a simmer / Simmer until the carrots are tender and the stock has almost evaporated / Add the liquorice and cook for a further 2 minutes, until it has just softened / Heat a frying pan, add the olive oil and little gem leaves and sauté until just wilted.

To serve

Place the little gems in the centre of your serving plates and spoon the carrots around the edge / Place the fish on top and spoon the bisque around the carrots.

Wine expert Susy Atkins's choice
Sainsbury's Taste the Difference Chablis
Chablis must be the ultimate fish-friendly white. I think this will deliver the buttery roundness that we want, but still end on an elegant, refreshing note. There are lovely apples and pears on the nose.

Dave Myers
Poached turbot with a lemon and kelp crust, served with a white wine and broad bean sauce on a bed of truffled wild mushrooms with crispy hasselback potatoes

Dave got his kelp from a fishmonger in Orkney but if you aren't lucky enough to be able to get hold of some, capers will work just as well.

Ingredients Serves 2

Potatoes
2 large potatoes, peeled
50g (2oz) melted butter

Turbot
110ml (4fl oz) chicken stock
110ml (4fl oz) dry white wine
Pinch of saffron
2 bay leaves
2 x 175g (6oz) turbot fillets
2 tablespoons ciabatta breadcrumbs
1 tablespoon chopped kelp or capers
Zest of 1 lemon
1 tablespoon lemon juice
25g (1oz) butter
150g (5oz) peeled broad beans (use frozen baby ones, let them thaw and the skin pops off brilliantly)
2 tablespoons crème fraîche

Mushrooms
2 tablespoons olive oil
1 garlic clove, crushed
125g (4½oz) wild mushrooms, little morels are good
2 teaspoons truffle oil

Method

Potatoes
Preheat the oven to 180°C/350°F/Gas 4 / Sit each potato into a tablespoon and cut lots of slices down through it – the edges of the spoon stop you cutting all the way through / Season and paint with melted butter / Place on a baking tray in the oven for 45 minutes or so until crispy, basting with more melted butter about halfway through.

Turbot
Shortly before the potatoes are due to be ready, place the stock, white wine, saffron and bay leaves in a shallow pan and bring to the boil / Add the fish and poach gently for 3 minutes / Lift out the fish, leaving the stock in the pan, and place on a baking tray / In a blender, blitz the breadcrumbs, kelp, lemon zest and juice and butter / Season to taste, then plaster over the fish / Place the fish in the oven for about 5 minutes / Meanwhile put the peeled broad beans into the fish stock residue and heat until reduced by half / Add the crème fraîche and season to taste.

Mushrooms
While the fish is in the oven, heat the olive oil in another frying pan and sweat the garlic for a minute / Add the mushrooms and fry gently for 3–4 minutes until just tender.

To serve

Dress the warm mushrooms with the truffle oil / Place half the mushrooms on each serving plate, with a fish portion on top / Dribble around the broad bean and wine sauce / Place the fan-shaped hasselback potatoes on the side.

Wine expert Olly Smith's choice
Verité Viognier
This wine has a lovely fresh zip that'll work superbly with the citrus zest in the recipe. It's also well rounded, which will pick up on the broad beans and crème fraîche.

Marcus Wareing
Roasted monkfish and chorizo hotpot

Marcus's precision comes through in this dish but you can present it in a more rustic style if you wish and it'll taste just as good.

Ingredients Serves 4

Broth
110g (4oz) yellow split peas
1 tablespoon vegetable oil
½ onion, diced
1 carrot, cut into 1cm (½ inch) cubes
1 garlic clove, crushed
½ leek, white part only, cut into 1cm (½ inch) pieces
110g (4oz) button mushrooms, diced
200g (7oz) semi-cured chorizo, cut into 1cm (½ inch) dice
50g (2oz) semi-dried tomatoes, chopped
1 tablespoon tomato purée
500ml (18fl oz) chicken stock
½ teaspoon salt
Bouquet garni of 2 bay leaves and ¼ bunch thyme

Monkfish
400g (14oz) monkfish tail, trimmed
1 tablespoon smoked paprika
1 tablespoon salt
1 tablespoon vegetable oil
50g (2oz) butter
200g (7oz) semi-cured chorizo, sliced thinly

To serve
¼ bunch of fresh flat-leaf parsley, chopped
Small handful of coriander cress
Extra virgin olive oil

Method

Broth
Place the split peas in a small saucepan and cover with cold water / Bring to a gentle simmer, then simmer until partly cooked but still slightly crunchy – about 10–12 minutes / Drain and set aside / Meanwhile, heat the vegetable oil gently in a medium-sized saucepan / Add the onion, carrot, garlic, leek, mushrooms, chorizo and tomatoes and cook gently so as to soften the vegetables, not colour them / After 5 minutes add the tomato purée, then add the stock, partly cooked yellow peas, salt, some black pepper and the bouquet garni / Allow to simmer very gently for 25–30 minutes, until the peas and vegetables are completely cooked through / Set aside while you cook the fish.

Monkfish
Cut the monkfish into 1cm (½ inch) thick slices / Mix the smoked paprika and salt together and lightly dust the monkfish with the mixture / Heat the oil in a medium-sized non-stick frying pan, add the butter, and when foaming, add the monkfish pieces / Colour the fish by spooning the butter over it until cooked through / Set aside, pour half of the butter out of the pan, then add the chorizo and cook until crispy.

To serve

Add the chopped parsley to the broth / Place 5–6 slices of monkfish in the centre of each serving bowl / Place a few slices of cooked chorizo on top and spoon over the broth / Garnish with the coriander cress and drizzle with extra virgin olive oil.

Wine expert Susie Barrie's choice
Tesco Finest Viña Mara Rioja Reserva
What this recipe needs is a good, fruity red wine that's elegant, but has just enough power to cope with the chorizo. This is fantastic – it's smoky and creamy and full of lovely plum and raspberry fruit flavours.

James Tanner
Smoked haddock and leek risotto with poached egg and mustard sauce

This classic combination of smoked fish and eggs makes a great dinner party dish.

Ingredients Serves 2

400g (14oz) natural smoked haddock fillet
1 litre (1¾ pints) fish stock
1 bay leaf
150g (5oz) butter
4 tablespoons olive oil
3 shallots, chopped
2 garlic cloves, finely chopped
200g (7oz) Arborio risotto rice
90ml (3½fl oz) dry vermouth
75g (3oz) Parmesan
1 leek, finely sliced
110ml (4fl oz) whipping cream
1 heaped teaspoon wholegrain mustard
50ml (2fl oz) white wine vinegar
2 eggs

Method

Remove the skin from the haddock and set aside / Place the skin in a saucepan with the fish stock and bay leaf and bring to a simmer / Heat a high-sided frying pan and add 50g (2oz) of the butter and 1 tablespoon of olive oil / Add the shallots and garlic and cook for 2 minutes, until just softened / Add the rice and cook for 1 minute, until toasted / Add the vermouth and cook until evaporated / Add the hot fish stock a ladleful at a time, stirring continuously, until all but 200ml (7fl oz) of the stock is absorbed and the rice is tender / Add 60g (2½oz) of the Parmesan and 25g (1oz) of butter, season with salt and black pepper and stir to combine / Heat a separate frying pan and add 50g (2oz) of the butter and the leek / Cook for 1–2 minutes, until just tender, then fold into the cooked risotto / Add half the remaining butter to the frying pan the leeks were cooked in, along with 1 tablespoon of olive oil / Add the smoked haddock and fry for 1–2 minutes on each side, until golden and heated through / Strain the remaining fish stock into a small saucepan, add the whipping cream and mustard and bring to a simmer / Bring a small pan of water to the boil and add the vinegar / Break the eggs into the pan and poach them for around 3½ minutes, until soft poached.

To serve

Place a spoonful of risotto in each serving bowl / Place a piece of haddock on top of the risotto and finish with a poached egg / Using a hand blender, froth the stock and mustard mixture and spoon around the haddock / Drizzle over the remaining olive oil and shave the rest of the Parmesan over.

Wine expert Susy Atkins's choice
Mâcon Villages Chardonnay
The flavour has a kind of buttery roundness, not heavy oak, and a very slight hint of nuttiness that will work well with the rather indulgent creamy elements and the smoked fish in this dish.

Lawrence Keogh
Pan-roasted ling with clams, perry and curly kale

Ling is a firm, white fish, a member of the cod family. If you can't get it, any similar white fish will work well in this recipe.

Ingredients Serves 2

Ling
4 tablespoons rapeseed oil
2 x 150g (5oz) ling fillets, skin on
300g (11oz) clams
200ml (7fl oz) perry (pear cider)
1 shallot, finely chopped
60g (2½oz) butter

Kale
110g (4oz) curly kale, stalks removed
60g (2½oz) butter
Zest of 1 lemon

To serve
2 teaspoons finely chopped fresh chives

Method

Ling
Preheat the oven to 190°C/375°F/Gas 5 / Heat a frying pan and add the rapeseed oil and ling fillets / Seal on each side until brown, then transfer the fish to a baking tray and place in the oven for 6–7 minutes, until just cooked / Remove from the oven and set aside to rest / Heat a saucepan and add the clams, perry and shallots / Cook, uncovered, for 2–3 minutes, until the clams have opened and the liquid has reduced down slightly / Drain the clams in a fine sieve and return the liquid to the pan / Bring back to the boil and cook until reduced and thickened / Whisk in the butter and season with salt and white pepper.

Kale
Meanwhile, bring a saucepan of salted water to the boil and add the curly kale / Cook for 2–3 minutes, until just tender / Drain and toss with the butter, lemon zest and some salt and white pepper.

To serve
Scatter the kale on your serving plates and place the fish on top / Finish the clams with a little more perry, to taste, and the chopped chives, stir through and spoon over the fish / Pour the sauce over the lot to finish.

Wine expert Peter Richards's choice
Les Piers Blancs Sauvignon Blanc
This is from the Loire, so you get a lovely fresh, crisp, delicious, crunchy sort of style. There's also quite a herbal quality to it, which is going to pick up nicely on the kale.

Silvena Rowe
Basil and kadaifi wrapped king prawns with pine nut tarator

James Martin
Hazelnut butter grilled scallops with salad

Richard Corrigan
Stuffed baby squid with chorizo and feta

Adam Byatt
Herb-crusted razor clams with garlic, chilli and lemon thyme

Nick Nairn
King prawn fritters with Romesco sauce

James Martin
Salt and pepper chilli squid with bok choi

Cyrus Todiwala
Keralan crab with currimbhoy salad

Prue Leith
Sweet and sour shrimp and pineapple soup

Sophie Grigson
Fregola con arselle (Sardinian pasta and clam soup)

James Martin
Thai green curried mussels

Dave Myers
Isle of Man queenie scallop pad thai

James Martin
Singapore chilli crab claws

Dave Myers
Kerala parathas and South Indian king prawns in coconut

Galton Blackiston
Velouté of Morston mussels

James Martin
Flambéd lobster

Sam Clark
Scallops with Oloroso sherry oyster mushrooms and migas

John Torode
Butternut squash and prawn curry with noodles

James Martin
Crab and chilli tagliatelle

Seafood

Silvena Rowe
Basil and kadaifi wrapped king prawns with pine nut tarator

This makes an impressive starter. Kadaifi pastry is similar to vermicelli pasta, but is normally used for sweet pastries in Mediterranean cooking.

Ingredients Serves 4

Prawns
12 large king prawns, shells and heads removed
2 tablespoons lemon juice
1 garlic clove, crushed
½ teaspoon ground coriander
½ tablespoon Tabasco sauce
24 large basil leaves
200g (7oz) kadaifi pastry

Tarator
1 slice of bread, crusts removed
200g (7oz) pine nuts
2 small garlic cloves, crushed
1 small bunch of fresh flat-leaf parsley, finely chopped
Juice of 1 lemon
5 tablespoons extra virgin olive oil

Method

Prawns
Put the prawns into a bowl with the lemon juice, garlic, coriander and Tabasco sauce and toss to coat / Place in the fridge and leave to marinate for 2 hours / Heat a deep-fat fryer to 170°C / Place a strand of the kadaifi pastry, about 10cm (4 inches) long, on a board and place 2 basil leaves on top / Place a king prawn on the pastry strand at one end, then start rolling until the prawn is covered in pastry – the kadaifi pastry is soft at this stage, so it is pliable and will stay wrapped / Repeat with the rest of the prawns, making sure that the pastry is covered while you are working so it doesn't dry out / Place the wrapped prawns in the deep-fat fryer and cook for 3–4 minutes, until the pastry is golden brown and the prawns are cooked through / Drain on kitchen paper and set aside to rest for 1 minute.

Tarator
While the prawns are marinating, put the bread into a bowl, cover with water, then squeeze out the excess / Place in a food processor with the pine nuts, garlic, parsley and lemon juice / Pulse to a smooth purée, then add the olive oil and purée once more / Season with salt and black pepper and refrigerate until needed.

To serve

Spoon 3 little piles of the tarator on to each serving plate and top with 3 prawns.

Wine expert Susie Barrie's choice
Tesco Finest Denman Vineyard Semillon
This is a style of wine that's relatively low in alcohol, just 10.5%, which makes it perfect for drinking with nibbly party food like this. It tastes really zesty and refreshing.

James Martin
Hazelnut butter grilled scallops with salad

Have a go at making your own flavoured butters – this is a great one to start with. They freeze really well.

Ingredients Serves 4

Butter
1 teaspoon olive oil
1 large shallot, finely sliced
150g (5oz) butter, softened
Zest of 1 lemon
2 tablespoons finely chopped fresh chervil
2 tablespoons finely chopped fresh chives
90g (3½oz) hazelnuts, finely chopped

Scallops
12 scallops, cleaned and returned to the curved half of the shell

Salad
1 tablespoon wholegrain mustard
1 tablespoon good white wine vinegar
3 tablespoons good rapeseed oil
2 little gem lettuces, leaves separated
1 punnet of pea shoots

Method

Butter
Heat a frying pan, add the olive oil and shallots and sweat until just softened / Place the butter in a bowl, then add the cooked shallots and all the remaining butter ingredients and mix thoroughly / Season with salt and black pepper and set aside.

Scallops
Preheat the grill to high / Place the scallops on a grill tray and top each one with a spoonful of butter / Place under the grill for 3-4 minutes, until just cooked through / Remove and set aside to rest for 1 minute.

Salad
Whisk the mustard, vinegar and oil together in a bowl and toss with the little gem leaves and pea shoots.

To serve

Place 3 scallops in their shells on each serving plate / Serve with a pile of salad alongside.

Richard Corrigan
Stuffed baby squid with chorizo and feta

You do need semi-cured chorizo for this dish. You can find it in a good Spanish or Portuguese deli. This fantastic recipe was a big hit in the studio.

Ingredients Serves 4

200g (7oz) semi-cured chorizo
150ml (5fl oz) white wine
200g (7oz) feta or feta-style cheese
20 baby squid tubes and tentacles, cleaned
A little vegetable oil
2 fennel heads, thinly sliced
1–2 tablespoons good extra virgin olive oil

Method

Preheat the oven to 180°C/350°F/Gas 4 / Put the chorizo into a saucepan with enough white wine to cover, bring to the boil, then reduce the heat and simmer for 15 minutes / Leave the chorizo to cool down in the pan, then peel away the skin / Chop the chorizo into small dice / Chop the cheese into similar-sized dice and mix with the chorizo in a bowl / Spoon the cheese and chorizo into the squid tubes, to about three-quarters full / Heat a large frying pan, add a film of oil, and when it is fiercely hot cook the squid in batches, searing them for 1 minute on one side, then turning them over for another minute (if you try to cook too many at once, they will boil and toughen, rather than sear) / As each one is done, transfer to an ovenproof dish or baking tray / When the last squid has been seared, add it to the rest and put the dish or tray into the oven for just 2 minutes / Add the tentacles to the frying pan and fry for 1–2 minutes, until just cooked / Bring a pan of salted water to the boil / Add the fennel and boil for 1 minute / Drain and toss with olive oil, salt and black pepper.

To serve

Pile the fennel into the centre of the serving plates and top with 5 squid each and a few tentacles / Drizzle with a little more olive oil and serve.

Wine expert Susy Atkins's choice
Campo Viejo Rioja Rosé
The Tempranillo grape used in this wine is the mainstay of many of Spain's reds and rosés. This is well balanced and has an aroma that just draws you in, with lots of red cherry and strawberry.

Adam Byatt
Herb-crusted razor clams with garlic, chilli and lemon thyme

Razor clams are becoming more widely available at fish counters but if you can't get them, make friends with a local fisherman and help him catch them on the beach!

Ingredients Serves 4

150g (5oz) butter
1 small bunch of lemon thyme, leaves picked
2 leeks, cut into 1cm (½ inch) dice, trimmings reserved
2 fennel heads, cut into 1cm (½ inch) dice, trimmings reserved
1 red chilli, deseeded and finely diced
3 garlic cloves, bashed
300ml (10fl oz) white wine
1kg (2lb 2oz) fresh razor clams, washed and drained
110g (4oz) breadcrumbs from sourdough bread
20g (¾oz) pecorino

To serve

Lime wedges

Method

Preheat the grill to high / Heat a heavy-based sauté pan, add half the butter, the lemon thyme, leeks, fennel, chilli and garlic and cook over a low heat until the vegetables soften / Heat a deep-sided sauté pan, add the remaining butter and the vegetable trimmings and cook for a few minutes / Add the white wine and cook until reduced by half, then add the clams / Cover with a lid and cook for 5 minutes, then drain the liquid into a jug / Add 200ml (7fl oz) of this cooking liquor to the fennel and leeks and cook until reduced by half / Remove the clams from their shells, slice the meat on an angle into 1cm (½ inch) pieces and add to the vegetables / Wash the shells and place on a baking tray, then spoon the mixture into the shells / Place the sourdough crumbs and pecorino in a food processor and blitz together / Sprinkle over the filled shells / Place under the grill until golden.

To serve

Serve with wedges of lime.

Wine expert Tim Atkin's choice
Single Estate Grenache Blanc, France
The acidity in this wine goes really well with the texture of the clams and the richness of the cheese. There's also a little sheen of oak in this wine, which goes very, very well with the toastiness of the baked breadcrumbs.

Nick Nairn
King prawn fritters with Romesco sauce

You can flash the peppers under a hot grill for a couple of minutes to get the same results as an open flame.

Ingredients Serves 4

Sauce

1 red pepper
2 wood-roasted peppers from a jar or tin
1 garlic clove, peeled and chopped
1 teaspoon sweet smoked paprika
½ teaspoon dried chilli flakes
100ml (3½fl oz) red wine vinegar
75g (3oz) flaked almonds, lightly toasted
200–250ml (7–9fl oz) extra virgin olive oil
1–2 tablespoons roughly chopped fresh flat-leaf parsley or coriander

Fritters

3 tablespoon self-raising flour
¼ teaspoon paprika
125g (4½oz) raw king prawns, shelled
1 tablespoon chopped shallots
1 tablespoon roughly chopped fresh flat-leaf parsley
2 tablespoons olive oil
90ml (3½fl oz) sparkling water or soda water

To serve

2 lemons, cut into wedges
1 bunch of micro greens

Method

Sauce

Roast the red pepper over an open gas flame until well charred and wrap in clingfilm to cool / When cold, remove the skin, stalk and seeds / Put both types of pepper, the garlic, sweet paprika, chilli flakes, vinegar and almonds into a food processor and season well with salt and black pepper / Blitz to a thick paste, scraping down the sides of the bowl with a spatula, then dribble in the oil with the motor running as if you were making mayonnaise, adding enough oil to give a thick but pourable consistency and adding a little hot water if it gets too thick / Stir in the parsley or coriander / This will keep in the fridge for up to 4 days, or freeze for up to 3 months.

Fritters

Sift the flour, paprika and a pinch of salt into a bowl / Roughly chop the prawns and stir into the mix with the shallots and parsley / Make a well in the centre and pour in the oil and two thirds of the water / Whisk the flour slowly into the liquid to form a smooth batter, adding more water if required, then set aside / Heat a deep-fat fryer to 180°C (or use a wok with enough oil to cover the fritters) / When the oil is hot enough, carefully lower the battered prawns into the oil, getting the spoon as close as you can to the hot oil, otherwise it will splatter / After about a minute, take the first fritters out of the basket and press them lightly, either with a big wad of kitchen paper or the back of a spoon – this flattens them and helps them cook through / Return the fritters to the oil for another 2 minutes, then lift and drain on kitchen paper / Season with salt.

To serve

Serve the fritters immediately they are cooked, with the Romesco sauce for dipping and lemon wedges to squeeze over / Pile some micro greens alongside.

Wine expert Susy Atkins's choice
Torres Viña Sol
This wine has a lovely citrus aroma, with a little bit of apples and pears in there too. It's not too grassy, and on the other hand it's not too tropical and fat either. It's a very easy-going wine, full of life.

James Martin
Salt and pepper chilli squid with bok choi

Speed is of the essence with this: the squid really does only take two minutes – no longer.

Ingredients Serves 4

Squid

½ teaspoon black peppercorns
½ teaspoon Sichuan peppercorns
1 teaspoon sea salt flakes
1–2 tablespoons sunflower oil
500g (1lb 2oz) squid, cleaned and cut into rings
1 red chilli, deseeded and thinly sliced
3 spring onions, sliced

Bok choi

4 heads of bok choi, roughly chopped
1 teaspoon vegetable oil
2 garlic cloves, finely sliced
1 red chilli, deseeded and finely sliced
2 tablespoons finely sliced fresh root ginger
2 spring onions, finely sliced
2 tablespoons toasted sesame oil

To serve

1 lime, quartered

Method

Squid

Heat a frying pan, then add the black peppercorns and Sichuan peppercorns and dry-roast them for a few seconds, shaking the pan now and then, until they darken slightly and become aromatic / Tip into a mortar and crush coarsely with the pestle, then stir in the sea salt flakes / Heat a wok over a high heat until smoking, then add half the oil and half the squid and stir-fry it for 2 minutes, until lightly coloured / Tip on to a plate, then cook the remaining squid in the same way / Return the first batch of squid to the wok and add half the salt and pepper mixture / Toss together for about 10 seconds, then add the red chilli and spring onions and toss together very briefly.

Bok choi

Meanwhile bring a pan of water to the boil / Place the bok choi in a steamer on top of the boiling water, cover and steam for 2–3 minutes / Heat a frying pan, add the vegetable oil, garlic, chilli, ginger and spring onions and stir-fry for 1 minute / Add the bok choi and sesame oil and toss to combine.

To serve

Pile the bok choi in the centre of each serving plate and top with the squid / Serve with a wedge of lime.

Wine expert Peter Richards's choice
Grove Mill Riesling

Cyrus Todiwala
Keralan crab with currimbhoy salad

It may seem as if there are a lot of ingredients here but, as with all Cyrus's dishes, everything comes together beautifully.

Ingredients Serves 4

Crab
1 tablespoon sunflower oil
1 teaspoon mustard seeds
2.5cm (1 inch) piece of fresh root ginger, peeled and finely diced
1 garlic clove, finely chopped
3–4 curry leaves, finely shredded
1 green chilli, deseeded and chopped
1 small dried red chilli, soaked in water, then drained and finely shredded
2 small shallots, finely diced
75g–110g (3–4oz) fresh coconut, grated
½ teaspoon red chilli powder
¼ teaspoon turmeric
200g (7oz) white crabmeat, picked over and all shell removed
1 plum tomato, deseeded and diced
1 tablespoon roughly chopped fresh coriander leaves

Salad
1 egg yolk
1 teaspoon white wine vinegar
½ teaspoon Dijon mustard
150ml (5fl oz) rapeseed oil
2 garlic cloves, finely chopped
2 green chillies, finely diced
3 tablespoons roughly chopped fresh coriander leaves
Juice of ½ lime
2 tablespoons olive oil
4 thin slices of white bread
4 hard-boiled eggs, roughly chopped into about 5mm (¼ inch) pieces
250g (9oz) Cos or any other large leafy lettuce, cut into 2.5cm (1 inch) pieces

Method

Crab
Make sure all the ingredients are prepared before you start cooking / In a wok or kadhai, add the oil and turn the heat up until it forms a haze / Add a couple of mustard seeds to check if they crackle immediately / If the oil is ready, add the mustard seeds and, if possible, cover the pan with a lid for a few moments to prevent the seeds flying all over the place / As soon as the crackling dies down and the aroma is that of something roasted, add the ginger, garlic, curry leaves and the green and red chillies / As soon as the garlic turns pale golden but not brown, add the shallots and continue to sauté until they turn soft / Add the coconut and sauté for 3–4 minutes, then add the chilli powder and ground turmeric / Sauté for about 30 seconds and add the crabmeat, tossing well for a further minute / Add the tomato and coriander and toss to combine / Check the seasoning.

Salad
Meanwhile, make the mayonnaise – place the egg yolk, vinegar and mustard into a food processor and blend until pale and creamy / With the motor running, pour in the rapeseed oil in a steady stream until the mayonnaise has thickened / Measure 200g (7oz) into a bowl, then add the garlic, chillies, coriander leaves and lime juice and mix thoroughly / Season with salt and black pepper / Heat a frying pan and add the olive oil / Dice the bread slices and add to the pan, season with salt and black pepper and toss together / Cook for 2–3 minutes, until golden and crispy on each side / Remove and drain on kitchen paper / Add the chopped eggs and lettuce leaves to the mayonnaise – do not over-mix, as the lettuce with go limp very rapidly / Stir in half the croutons, reserving the remainder.

To serve
Pile the salad into individual bowls and top with the rest of the croutons / Spoon the crab alongside and serve immediately.

Wine expert Susie Barrie's choice
Vin D'Alsace Gewürztraminer
Gewürztraminer is a wine with soft acidity and usually just a tiny touch of sweetness, and that makes it the ultimate wine to drink with curry. It's so scented and heady, fantastic.

Prue Leith
Sweet and sour shrimp and pineapple soup

This is essentially chicken stock with lots of lovely ingredients added, so don't cheat with this one – the fresh stock does make a difference.

Ingredients Serves 4

Stock
1 chicken, preferably a stewing hen, whole or cut up
1cm (½ inch) piece of fresh root ginger, thinly sliced
2 leeks, white part only, thickly sliced

Soup
2–3 tablespoons vegetable oil
2 small tomatoes, preferably slightly unripe, peeled and quartered
2 tablespoons Thai fish sauce
2 tablespoons lemon juice
2 starfruit, preferably slightly unripe, thinly sliced
1 small pineapple, preferably slightly unripe, cut into chunks
½ teaspoon ground black pepper
2 tablespoons tamarind purée
1–2 teaspoons caster sugar
500ml (18fl oz) homemade chicken stock (see above) or bought fresh chicken stock
3 spring onions, including green parts, thinly sliced
1kg (2lb 2oz) raw king prawns, shelled and deveined
Large handful of coriander leaves, roughly chopped
1 long fresh red chilli, deseeded and sliced thinly

Method

Stock
Rinse the chicken well under running water / Place in a stockpot and add cold water to just cover, about 1–1.5 litres (2½ pints) / Bring to the boil, uncovered, over a medium heat / Skim to remove any foam, then add the ginger and leeks / Reduce the heat to a simmer and cook until the stock is well flavoured, about 1½ hours (and up to 3 hours) / Strain and cool.

Soup
Place a large saucepan on the heat and add the oil and half the tomatoes / Cook for 3 minutes, until the tomatoes have just softened and are becoming watery / Add the fish sauce, lemon juice, starfruit and pineapple and stir well / Add the pepper, tamarind, and sugar to taste / Add the stock, spring onions and remaining tomatoes, then bring to a rolling boil and boil for 2 minutes / Add the prawns and cook for 1 minute / Remove from the heat and stir in the coriander leaves and chilli slices / Serve immediately.

Wine expert Olly Smith's choice
Dr Wagner Ockfener Bockstein Riesling
This is like a juicy nectarine at the height of summer – the wine tastes a little sweet, but the heat of the dish will tone down the sugar and emphasise the dazzling freshness in the glass.

Sophie Grigson
Fregola con arselle
(Sardinian pasta and clam soup)

Fregola are semolina-based beads of pasta and work particularly well with seafood.

Ingredients Serves 6

1kg (2lb 2oz) small clams, rinsed
Large pinch of saffron
4 tablespoons extra virgin olive oil, plus extra to serve
3 garlic cloves, sliced
4 tablespoons chopped fresh parsley
¼ teaspoon chilli flakes
1.2 litres (2 pints) fish stock
4 medium tomatoes, peeled, deseeded and diced
250g (9oz) fregola
Finely grated zest of 1 lemon

Method

Rinse the clams thoroughly and drain / Put the saffron in a cup with a tablespoon of hot water and set aside / Heat the olive oil in a wide saucepan and add the garlic, parsley and chilli / Stir around for about 1 minute / Add the stock and half the tomatoes and bring up to the boil / Add the fregola and simmer for 10 minutes, stirring frequently, until the pasta is just cooked / Meanwhile, pour enough water into a large pan to cover the bottom by about 5mm (¼ inch) / Bring to the boil, add the clams, then cover tightly with a lid and shake over a high heat until all the clams have opened, about 5 minutes / Lift them out with a slotted spoon, discarding any that have not opened / Carefully pour off most of the cooking liquor, leaving behind the sandy grit that will have settled on the bottom of the pan / Add the clams to the saucepan of simmering pasta and stock along with their cooking liquor, the saffron, lemon zest and remaining tomatoes / Take off the heat and serve immediately, drizzling a little olive oil into each bowl of soup.

Wine expert Susie Barrie's choice
Marotti Campi Luzano
This is a really classic Verdicchio, dry and refreshing, with lovely floral and lemon rind flavours It's got exactly the right vibrancy and earthy quality we need to match this dish.

James Martin
Thai green curried mussels

This makes a nice change from the usual wine-based mussel dishes.

Ingredients Serves 4

Paste

3 lemongrass stalks, roughly chopped

4–6 green bird's-eye chillies, deseeded and chopped

3 garlic cloves, roughly chopped

5cm (2 inch) piece of fresh galangal or root ginger, peeled and chopped

2 lime leaves, roughly chopped

2 Thai shallots, chopped

4 tablespoons chopped fresh coriander root

1 teaspoon ground cumin

1 teaspoon ground coriander

½ teaspoon crushed black pepper

1 tablespoon Thai fish sauce

Mussels

1 tablespoon vegetable oil

1kg (2lb 2oz) mussels, cleaned

400ml (14fl oz) coconut milk

Juice of 1 lime

2 tablespoons roughly chopped fresh coriander

2 tablespoons roughly chopped Thai basil

Method

Paste
Place all the ingredients into a food processor and blitz to a purée.

Mussels
Heat a wok, add the oil and 2 tablespoons of the paste and cook for 1 minute / Add the mussels and the coconut milk / Cover and bring to the boil, then simmer for 2–3 minutes, until the mussels are opened / Discard any mussels that have not opened, add the lime juice and herbs and serve immediately.

Dave Myers
Isle of Man queenie scallop pad thai

Queenie scallops are so highly revered on the Isle of Man that they have a week-long festival to celebrate them.

Ingredients Serves 4

Paste
4 dried red chillies, deseeded
1 small shallot, diced
3 garlic cloves
1 tablespoon chopped fresh galangal
2 lemongrass stalks, outer leaves removed, finely chopped
Zest of 1 lime
2 teaspoons roughly chopped fresh coriander (use the root if you can)
½ teaspoon white peppercorns
1 teaspoon coriander seeds
½ teaspoon cumin seeds
2 teaspoons Thai shrimp paste

Pad thai
200g (7oz) dried flat rice noodles
3 tablespoons groundnut oil
2 teaspoons rice vinegar
½ onion, chopped
1 tablespoon chopped fresh root ginger
2 tablespoons Thai fish sauce
1 tablespoon light soy sauce
150g (5oz) fresh bean sprouts
2 spring onions, finely sliced
110g (4oz) pak choi, finely sliced
500g (1lb 2oz) queenie scallops
200g (7oz) raw king prawns, shelled

To serve
50g (2oz) roasted peanuts, crushed
2 limes, cut into wedges

Method

Paste
Place all the ingredients into a pestle and mortar and grind to a smooth red paste (this will take a while but it does somehow taste better if it's done by hand – you can use a coffee grinder) / This will make about 4 times more than you need, so put what you don't use in a sterilised jar, cover with oil and seal / It will keep in the fridge for up to 2 weeks.

Pad thai
Put the noodles into hot, but not boiling, water to soak for 10 minutes / Refresh under cold water, then drain and place in a bowl / Add 1 tablespoon of the groundnut oil and the rice vinegar and mix well – the oil and vinegar will stop the noodles sticking together / Heat a wok, add the remaining oil, the onion and ginger and cook until soft / Add 2 teaspoons of your curry paste and cook for a further 2 minutes then add the Thai fish sauce and light soy sauce / Add the noodles and coat well with the curry paste mixture / Add the bean sprouts, spring onions and pak choi and cook for 2–3 minutes / Meanwhile, heat a frying pan, add 1 teaspoon of groundnut oil, then add the scallops and prawns and cook for 1 minute / Add the scallops and prawns to the noodles in the wok and stir in.

To serve

Serve garnished with the crushed roasted peanuts and the lime wedges.

Wine expert Olly Smith's choice
Ken Forrester Chenin Blanc
This wine is sunshine in a bottle. It's going to work perfectly because it's got lovely lashings of tropical fruit and a refreshing kick that will work with the heat of the dish.

James Martin
Singapore chilli crab claws

There is some controversy about where this dish originates from, Singapore or Malaysia, but one thing's not debatable, it's fantastic.

Ingredients Serves 2–4

16 raw crab claws, cracked
3cm (1¼ inch) piece of fresh
    root ginger, finely shredded
2 garlic cloves, chopped
3 red bird's-eye chillies,
    deseeded and finely
    chopped
125ml (4½ fl oz) tomato sauce
75ml (3fl oz) sweet chilli sauce
75ml (3fl oz) hoisin sauce
3 tablespoons Thai fish sauce
75ml (3fl oz) water
1 tablespoon caster sugar

Method

Heat a frying pan and add the crab claws / Cook for 1 minute, then add the ginger, garlic and chillies and stir-fry for 2 minutes / Whisk the tomato, sweet chilli, hoisin and fish sauces together in a bowl, then add the water and sugar and stir to combine / Pour over the crab and toss, then bring to a simmer and cover with a lid / Cook for 8–10 minutes, until the crab is cooked through and the sauce is sticky / Remove the crab from the pan and serve, cracking the claws to release the meat.

Dave Myers
Kerala parathas and South Indian king prawns in coconut

Practise your parathas! Allow yourself some time to get these flatbreads right, as they can be tricky at first, but don't give up – they're worth it.

Ingredients Serves 4

Parathas
500g (1lb 2oz) plain white flour
2 eggs, beaten
1 teaspoon caster sugar
1 teaspoon salt
2 tablespoons condensed milk
150ml (5fl oz) milk
110g (4oz) butter, melted
2 tablespoons sunflower oil

Prawns
500g (1lb 2oz) jumbo tiger prawns, shelled but tails retained
1 onion, roughly chopped
1 red chilli, deseeded
2 garlic cloves
1 thumb-sized piece of fresh root ginger, peeled
2 tablespoons sunflower oil
12 fresh curry leaves
1 teaspoon black mustard seeds
½ teaspoon methi powder (ground fenugreek)
Pinch of asafoetida
1 tablespoon water
½ teaspoon turmeric
200ml (7fl oz) coconut milk
Juice of 1 lime

To serve
4 tablespoons finely chopped fresh coriander leaves
1 lime, cut into wedges

Method

Parathas
Place the flour, eggs, sugar, salt and condensed milk in a food processor fitted with a dough blade / Process, gradually adding the milk, until a soft dough is formed / Wrap the dough in clingfilm and set aside to chill in the fridge for about an hour / Take the dough from the fridge and pull off a piece about the size of a lime / Roll it into a ball, then roll it out as thin as you can / Paint on to the dough a coating of melted butter, using a pastry brush / Starting at one side, pleat the dough in about 1cm (½ inch) pleats like a fan / Roll the pleated dough around itself like a Catherine wheel and tuck the end into the middle / Squeeze this into a ball and roll out until the disc is about 5mm (¼ inch) thick and about 15 cm (6 inches) across / Roll out the remaining parathas in the same manner / Heat a frying pan, add the sunflower oil and the parathas and cook for about 1 minute each side, until golden and crispy / The buttered pleats will act like puff pastry, making the parathas crisp on the outside and soft and flaky on the inside / Keep the parathas warm in a low oven while you prepare and cook the prawns.

Prawns
Slice the prawns nearly in half lengthways, leaving the body attached to the tail, and devein / Put the onion, chilli, garlic and ginger into a food processor and blitz to form a paste / Heat a sauté pan, add the oil, curry leaves, mustard seeds, methi powder and asafoetida, and cook for about 30 seconds / Add the oniony paste and continue cooking for a couple of minutes / Add the water, turmeric and prawns and cook until the prawns are well covered with the spices and they have started to change colour / Add the coconut milk, season with salt and black pepper and simmer for a couple of minutes just to cook the prawns through / Add a little lime juice and check the seasoning – this is meant to be quite a dry curry.

To serve
Place the golden parathas to one side of your serving plate / Add a heap of the spicy coconut prawns / Garnish with the chopped coriander and the lime wedges.

Wine expert Susy Atkins's choice
Sainsbury's Taste the Difference Chilean Sauvignon Blanc
We want a dry, aromatic white with a kind of green, herbaceous edge to it. This has green fruit on the scent, lots of lime and gooseberry. It's so bracing, it really wakes up your whole mouth.

Galton Blackiston
Velouté of Morston mussels

These particular mussels are local to Galton in Norfolk and he loves them, but you can use any kind.

Ingredients Serves 6

4kg (7.5Ib) Morston mussels, scraped, de-bearded, thoroughly cleaned and rinsed in plenty of cold running water
225ml (8fl oz) white wine
1 medium onion, finely sliced
50g (2oz) butter
2 teaspoons plain flour
1 teaspoon medium curry powder
150ml (5fl oz) double cream
1 pack of baby leaf spinach

To serve

Plenty of chopped chives
Crusty bread

Method

Heat a large pan over a high heat and quickly throw in the mussels and the white wine / Put a lid on the saucepan and keep it over a high heat, shaking the pan until all the mussels have opened / Drain them in a large colander over a bowl to catch the liquor / Remove the mussels from their shells, discarding any that have not opened, and set aside / In another pan, cook the onions in the butter until soft / Stir in the flour and curry powder and cook gently for a few minutes / Stir in the liquor that the mussels were cooked in, making sure it is thoroughly incorporated, and simmer for 10 minutes / Add the cream, bring back to the boil and add the mussels / Add the spinach and cook for a further 1 minute.

To serve

Ladle the mussels into warmed bowls, sprinkle liberally with chopped chives and serve with crusty bread.

Wine expert Peter Richards's choice
Soave Superiore Classico Cantina di Monteforte
A good tip with Soave is to look for the words 'Superiore Classico' on the label, as this indicates more intensity and character in the wine. There are loads of lovely citrusy, almondy and creamy spicy aromas in this wine.

James Martin
Flambéd lobster

Lobster would be a lot of people's choice for 'food heaven', so James was under pressure to do it justice when he cooked this dish on the show.

Ingredients Serves 4

Fish stock
250g (9oz) white fish trimmings, rinsed
2 leeks, white part only, roughly chopped
½ head fennel, roughly chopped
2 carrots, roughly chopped
1 bay leaf

Lobster
1 tablespoon olive oil
2 shallots, finely chopped
1 garlic clove, finely chopped
2 tinned plum tomatoes, drained and finely chopped
2 cooked lobsters, split, tail and claw meat removed
75ml (3fl oz) brandy
50g (2oz) butter
3 tablespoons roughly chopped fresh chervil

Method

Fish stock
Put all the ingredients into a saucepan and cover with cold water / Place on the heat and bring to the boil / Simmer for 25 minutes, skimming off any froth that comes to the surface / Strain into a container and reserve / The stock can be frozen.

Lobster
Heat a sauté pan, add the olive oil, shallots and garlic and cook for 2 minutes / Add the tomatoes and sauté for 1 minute / Add the lobsters and the brandy / Ignite and flame the brandy, tossing the lobster to coat / Add 110ml (4fl oz) of the fish stock and simmer for 2 minutes / Add the butter and chervil and season with salt and black pepper.

Sam Clark
Scallops with Oloroso sherry, oyster mushrooms and migas

Sam Clark is known for the brilliant North African food he serves at his restaurant, Moro. This recipe is a great example of his style.

Ingredients Serves 4

Migas
6 tablespoons olive oil
10 garlic cloves
200g (7oz) day-old, slightly dry, rustic white bread, such as ciabatta or sourdough, crusts removed, torn in 2cm (¾ inch) pieces
2 bay leaves
40 saffron strands (a large pinch), infused in 3½ tablespoons boiling water

Scallops
5 tablespoons olive oil
½ large onion, finely chopped
12 large scallops with corals, out of their shell, washed, trimmed of the tough side muscle and patted dry
150ml (6fl oz) medium dry Oloroso sherry
25ml (1fl oz) water

Mushrooms
300g (11fl oz) oyster mushrooms, torn into strips if large
1 tablespoon olive oil

To serve
1 tablespoon fresh roughly chopped oregano
1 teaspoon sweet paprika

Method

Migas
Heat the olive oil in a wide frying pan or saucepan over a low to medium heat / Add the whole garlic cloves and fry for a few minutes to release the flavour – reduce the heat if the garlic is sizzling too quickly, as it is very important that it does not burn / Now add the bread and bay leaves and fry gently for 20–25 minutes, turning and stirring often, until the bread and garlic are golden all over / Pour over the saffron and its water and continue to cook for 5–10 minutes, until the bread is crunchy again / Remove from the heat, season with salt and keep warm.

Scallops
While the migas are cooking, place a small saucepan over a medium heat and add 3 tablespoons of the olive oil / When hot, stir in the onion and a small pinch of salt and fry for about 15–20 minutes, stirring occasionally, until golden brown, caramelised and sweet in flavour – if the onion is colouring too quickly, turn down the heat / Drain off any excess oil and set aside / Set a frying pan over a high heat and add the remaining 2 tablespoons of olive oil / When it is hot add the scallops, seasoned with a little salt and black pepper / Sear the scallops for 1–2 minutes on each side, until just golden brown / Add the softened onion, sherry and water, taking care it does not spit too much, and gently simmer for another minute.

Mushrooms
Get a griddle pan very hot / Toss the mushrooms with the olive oil and season with salt and black pepper / Place on the griddle and cook for 1–2 minutes, until scored and cooked through.

To serve

Spread the mushrooms on serving plates / Dot the scallops among the mushrooms, followed by the crisp migas, soft garlic and Oloroso sauce / Scatter the oregano on top and sprinkle generously with paprika.

Wine expert Olly Smith's choice
Laurenz und Sophie Singing Grüner Veltliner
Austria's signature Grüner Veltliner is great with all shellfish but magnificent with scallops. This wine is all about texture, and you've also got that peppery kick to match up to the Oloroso sherry.

John Torode
Butternut squash and prawn curry with noodles

The lime pickle is essential to balance out the sweetness in this dish.

Ingredients Serves 3–4

Curry
150ml (5fl oz) vegetable oil
50g (2oz) red curry paste
15g (⅔oz) palm sugar
1 medium butternut squash, peeled and cut into large chunks, about 4–5cm (1½–2 inches)
1 sweet potato, peeled and cut into large chunks, about 4–5cm (1½–2 inches)
400ml (14fl oz) coconut milk
90ml (3½fl oz) coconut cream
½ tablespoon Thai fish sauce
2 lemongrass stalks, crushed
1 tablespoon lime pickle
250g (9oz) raw king prawns, shelled and deveined
250g (9oz) Ming or egg noodles, precooked

Garnish
A little vegetable oil
50g (2oz) red chilli, deseeded and thinly sliced
50g (2oz) garlic, thinly sliced
50g (2oz) shallots, thinly sliced

To serve
50g (2oz) beansprouts, picked and washed
Small bunch of fresh coriander, leaves picked
Small bunch of fresh basil, leaves picked

Method

Curry
Heat 75ml (3fl oz) of the oil and add the red curry paste / Fry for 2 minutes, then add the palm sugar and let it cook with the curry paste for 4 minutes until sticky and fragrant / Add the butternut squash and sweet potato, stir well and cook for 2–3 minutes / Pour in the coconut milk and the coconut cream, season with the fish sauce and add the lemongrass / Bring to the boil and cook for about 20–30 minutes over a medium heat until the squash and potato are soft but not mushy / Add the lime pickle and prawns and cook for a further 2 minutes, until the prawns have cooked through / Cook the noodles according to the packet instructions.

Garnish
While the squash and sweet potato are cooking, heat some oil in a wok and add the sliced chillies / Cook slowly over a gentle heat until all the moisture from the chillies has evaporated (at which point the oil will stop bubbling), then increase the heat slightly, so that they caramelise and crisp up, but without turning too dark / Remove and repeat the process with the garlic and then the shallots.

To serve

Pile the noodles into shallow serving bowls / Top with several spoonfuls of butternut and prawn curry / Toss together the beansprouts, coriander and basil and pile on top of the curry / Finish with a handful of the fried chilli, garlic and shallot.

Wine expert Olly Smith's choice
Ken Forrester Chenin Blanc

James Martin
Crab and chilli tagliatelle

Crab is another personal 'food heaven' ingredient for James, and this simple homemade pasta dish is a wonderful way to serve it.

Ingredients Serves 4

Pasta
200g (7oz) 'OO' flour
1 whole egg
6 egg yolks
50g (2oz) fine semolina flour

Sauce
1 tablespoon olive oil
2 shallots, finely chopped
1 red chilli, deseeded and
   finely sliced
½ lemongrass stalk, finely
   chopped
3cm (1¼ inch) piece of fresh
   root ginger, finely chopped
1 teaspoon hot curry powder
200ml (7fl oz) white wine
250ml (9fl oz) double cream
350g (12oz) picked brown and
   white crabmeat
Juice of 1 lime
3 tablespoons finely chopped
   fresh coriander

To serve

Lime wedges

Method

Pasta
Place the flour, egg and yolks in a food processor and process for 1 minute until everything is bound together / Wrap in clingfilm and place in the fridge to rest for 30 minutes / Divide the pasta in half and pass each piece through the pasta machine several times, gradually reducing the thickness, until it feels elastic / Add the tagliatelle cutter to the pasta machine and pass the pasta through to form 5mm (¼ inch) strips / Dust with the semolina flour and either use it straight away or cover and place in the fridge overnight to firm up (this will make it easier to handle) / When ready to cook the pasta, bring a large pan of salted water to the boil, add the tagliatelle and cook for 2–3 minutes, until tender, then drain and return it to the pan.

Sauce
While the water for the pasta is coming to the boil, heat a frying pan and add the olive oil, shallots, chilli, lemongrass, ginger and curry powder / Fry for 2–3 minutes, then add the white wine and bring to a simmer / Cook until the wine has reduced by half, then add the cream / Cook for a further minute, then add the crabmeat / Stir to combine thoroughly and simmer for 1 minute / Season with salt and black pepper, then add the lime juice and coriander / Add the crab sauce to the pan with the pasta and toss to combine.

To serve

Spoon into shallow bowls, and serve with wedges of lime.

Wine expert Olly Smith's choice
Laurent Miquel Nord Sud Viognier

James Martin
Goat's cheese and shallot tarte tatin with salad

James Martin
Watercress soup with crushed Jersey Royals and chives

James Martin
Onion bhajis with mango chutney

Stuart Gillies
Risotto of violet artichokes with artichoke salad

James Martin
Chestnut and wild mushroom tagliarini

Adam Byatt
Hazelnut gnocchi with girolles, crisp fried duck egg and Parmesan

James Martin
Pumpkin and amaretti tortellini with tomato and basil sauce

Vegetarian

James Martin
Goat's cheese and shallot tarte tatin with salad

All this dish needs is sunshine and you've got the perfect summer lunch.

Ingredients Serves 2

Tatin
50g (2oz) butter
2 teaspoons caster sugar
2 sprigs of fresh thyme
3 banana shallots, peeled and halved lengthways
250g (9oz) ready-made puff pastry, rolled to 5mm (¼ inch) thick
75g (3oz) soft goat's cheese
200g (7oz) firm goat's cheese

Dressing
25g (1oz) honey
2 tablespoons truffle oil
1 tablespoon extra virgin olive oil
Juice of ½ lemon

Salad
1 punnet of micro cress
50g (2oz) lamb's lettuce

Method

Tatin
Preheat the oven to 200°C/400°F/Gas 6 / Heat 2 small ovenproof blini pans, then add half the butter and half the sugar to each and brown slightly / Add the sprigs of thyme and the shallots, placing 2 halves cut side down and one half cut side up in each pan / Cook for 3–4 minutes, until they just begin to brown / Place the rolled-out pastry on a clean, floured surface and crumble the soft goat's cheese over half the pastry / Fold the pastry over and roll to 5mm (¼ inch) thick once more / Cut out 2 circles slightly larger than the circumference of the blini pans / Cover each pan with a pastry round, pushing the edge down around the shallots / Transfer to the oven and bake for 15–20 minutes, until the pastry is golden brown and cooked through / Remove from the oven and set aside to cool slightly.

Dressing
Meanwhile place the honey and oils in a small bowl and whisk to combine / Add the lemon juice and season with salt and black pepper.

Salad
Put the salad leaves into a bowl and toss with a little of the dressing.

To serve

Preheat the grill to high / Slice the firm goat's cheese in half and place on a grill tray / Place under the grill for 2 minutes until golden / Turn the tatin out into the centre of the plate / Top with the grilled goat's cheese and a small ball of dressed salad / Spoon a little of the remaining dressing around the edge of the plate.

Wine expert Peter Richards's choice
La Brille Sauvignon Blanc

James Martin
Watercress soup with crushed Jersey Royals and chives

Peppery watercress goes fantastically well with new Jersey Royals – make the most of them when they are both in season from April.

Ingredients Serves 4

Soup
50g (2oz) butter
2 large banana shallots, roughly chopped
125g (4½oz) Jersey Royal potatoes, washed, scrubbed and thinly sliced
450ml (16fl oz) vegetable stock
225g (8oz) watercress, roughly chopped, plus extra for serving
150ml (5fl oz) double cream
Pinch of freshly grated nutmeg

Jersey Royals
400g (14oz) Jersey Royal potatoes, washed and scrubbed
75g (3oz) butter
4 tablespoons finely chopped fresh chives
110ml (4fl oz) double cream
Juice of ½ lemon

Method

Soup
Heat a large saucepan, add the butter and shallots and fry for 2 minutes, until just softened / Add the potatoes and stock, bring to a simmer and cook for 5 minutes, until the potatoes are just tender / Add the watercress and simmer for 2 minutes / Place in a blender or food processor and blitz to a purée / Return the purée to the saucepan and add the cream / Season with salt, black pepper and the nutmeg.

Jersey Royals
Place the potatoes in a saucepan and cover with water / Bring to the boil and cook for 8–10 minutes, until tender / Drain and return to the saucepan / Add the butter and chives and crush the potatoes with the back of a fork / Meanwhile, pour the cream into a bowl, add the lemon juice, salt and black pepper, and whisk to soft peaks.

To serve
Pile the potatoes into the centre of a soup plate / Ladle the soup around the potatoes / Top with a spoonful of soured cream and a few sprigs of watercress.

Wine expert Peter Richards's choice
Oxford Landing Viognier

James Martin
Onion bhajis with mango chutney

These bhajis are so simple to make and much healthier than a takeaway.

Ingredients Serves 4

Chutney

1 teaspoon black mustard seeds
1 teaspoon black peppercorns
1 teaspoon cumin seeds
1 teaspoon dried chilli flakes
1 teaspoon coriander seeds
1 green mango, peeled and sliced
2 ripe mangoes, peeled and sliced
125g (4½oz) light soft brown sugar
110ml (4fl oz) malt vinegar

Bhajis

2 teaspoons cumin seeds
2 teaspoons coriander seeds
2 black cardamom pods, split
2 teaspoons black mustard seeds
2 teaspoons yellow mustard seeds
2 dried chillies, roughly chopped
1 teaspoon salt
1 onion, sliced
110g (4oz) gram (chickpea) flour
Juice of 1 lemon
4 tablespoons water
1 small bunch of fresh coriander, chopped

To serve

1 lemon, quartered

Method

Chutney

Heat a frying pan, then add all the spices and toast for 30 seconds, until the mustard seeds start to pop / Add the green and ripe mangoes and cook for a further minute / Add the sugar and cook until dissolved, then add the vinegar / Cover and simmer for 25 minutes, until the mixture has thickened and the mango has broken down / Place half the chutney into a food processor and blitz to a purée, then return it to the pan and stir to combine / Pour into sterilised airtight jars and set aside to cool.

Bhajis

When the chutney is ready, heat a deep-fat fryer to 190°C / Place all the spices and salt in a pestle and mortar and grind until quite fine / Place the ground spices in a bowl with the onions and gram flour and stir thoroughly to combine / Add the lemon juice and water and mix well to form a very sticky batter / Add the coriander and a pinch of black pepper and mix once more / Drop spoonfuls into the deep-fat fryer and cook for 2–3 minutes, until golden and crispy / Drain on kitchen paper.

To serve

Place a few bhajis on a plate and squeeze over the lemon juice / Spoon a dollop of mango chutney on the side.

Stuart Gillies
Risotto of violet artichokes with artichoke salad

Violet artichokes grow in abundance in Provence and can be eaten raw when young. They are delicious in this risotto.

Ingredients Serves 4

Stock
2 tablespoons olive oil
2 onions, roughly chopped
3 carrots, roughly chopped
½ head of celery, roughly
  chopped
½ celeriac, roughly chopped
2 leeks, roughly chopped
½ head fennel, roughly
  chopped
1 head garlic, cut in half
4 white peppercorns
1 small bunch of fresh thyme
1 small bunch of fresh
  rosemary
1 small bunch of fresh flat-leaf
  parsley

Risotto
1 litre (1¾ pints) of the
  vegetable stock (see above)
2 tablespoons olive oil
75g (3oz) butter
1 shallot, finely chopped
1 garlic clove, crushed
1 teaspoon finely chopped
  fresh thyme leaves
250g (9oz) Carnaroli risotto rice
50ml (2fl oz) white wine
2 baby violet artichokes,
  trimmed
25g (1oz) mascarpone
50g (2oz) Parmesan, freshly
  grated

Dressing
1 tablespoon white wine vinegar
1 teaspoon English mustard
3 tablespoons extra virgin
  olive oil

Salad
½ head of curly endive
2 baby violet artichokes,
  trimmed
Juice of ½ lemon

Method

Stock
Heat a large stockpot and add the olive oil / Add all the vegetables and the peppercorns and cook for 5 minutes / Cover with water, bring to the boil, then simmer for 15 minutes / Add the herbs and cook for a further 5 minutes / Turn off the heat and set aside to cool in the pan / When cool, place in the fridge overnight if not using immediately / Strain when ready to make the risotto.

Risotto
Pour 1 litre (1¾ pints) of the stock into a pan, place on the heat and bring to a simmer / Heat a sauté pan and add the olive oil and half the butter / Add the shallots, garlic and thyme and cook for 2 minutes / Add the rice and cook for 1 minute, until just starting to toast / Add the white wine and cook until almost all has been absorbed / Gradually add the hot stock, several ladlefuls at a time, stirring all the time / Continue to cook until the rice is just tender and nearly all the stock has been absorbed / Finely slice the artichokes (either by hand or on a mandolin) / Add to the risotto and cook for 2–3 minutes with the last of the stock / Add the mascarpone, the remaining butter and the Parmesan and stir to combine / Season with salt and black pepper.

Dressing
Whisk together the white wine vinegar, mustard and olive oil and season with salt and black pepper.

Salad
When the risotto is almost ready, slice the artichokes very thinly and place in a bowl with the endive and lemon juice / Toss the salad in the dressing.

To serve

Spoon the risotto into the centre of each serving plate / Top with a ball of the salad.

Wine expert Susie Barrie's choice
Grechetto di Todi
We're looking for a white wine to go with this, and this one has great acidity and a really lovely, lemony tang. It also has a herbal note that will complement those lovely fresh thyme flavours.

James Martin
Chestnut and wild mushroom tagliarini

The autumnal flavours of chestnuts and wild mushrooms work perfectly together in this pasta dish.

Ingredients Serves 4

Chestnuts
300g (11oz) chestnuts in their shells

Mushrooms
50g (2oz) butter
2 shallots, finely chopped
200g (7oz) wild mushrooms
50ml (2fl oz) brandy
175ml (6fl oz) double cream

Tagliarini
500g (1lb 2oz) fresh tagliarini

To serve

2 tablespoons finely chopped fresh flat-leaf parsley
2 tablespoons finely chopped fresh chervil
25g (1oz) Parmesan, freshly grated

Method

Chestnuts
Preheat the oven to 220°C/425°F/Gas 7 / Pierce the chestnuts with a knife, making a small slit in the shell (this prevents them exploding) / Lay them on a baking tray and place in the oven for 20–25 minutes, until tender / Cool, then peel and roughly chop.

Mushrooms
Heat a frying pan, add the butter and shallots and cook for 1–2 minutes / Add the mushrooms and fry for a further minute / Add the brandy and flame to burn off the alcohol / Add the cream and chestnuts, bring to a simmer and cook for 2 minutes.

Tagliarini
Meanwhile, bring a large pan of salted water to the boil, add the pasta and cook according to the packet instructions.

To serve

Drain the pasta and add it to the sauce, along with the parsley, chervil and Parmesan / Season with salt and black pepper, and toss well to combine.

Adam Byatt
Hazelnut gnocchi with girolles, crisp fried duck egg and Parmesan

Hazelnut makes a clever addition to these classic gnocchi. If you can't get girolles use whatever mushrooms you can find.

Ingredients Serves 4

Gnocchi
225g (8oz) dry mashed potato
1 egg
4 teaspoons hazelnut oil
50g (2oz) whole skinned hazelnuts, roasted and crushed
100g (3¾oz) 'OO' pasta flour

Sauce
2 tablespoons olive oil
300g (11oz) girolle mushrooms
5 sprigs of fresh thyme, leaves picked
2 large shallots, thinly sliced
200ml (7fl oz) vegetable stock
50g (2oz) butter
4 duck eggs

To serve
8 whole roasted hazelnuts
1 punnet of fresh parsley shoots
100g (3¾oz) aged Parmesan

Method

Gnocchi
Place the mashed potato, egg, hazelnut oil and crushed hazelnuts in a bowl and mix well / Add the flour a few spoonfuls at a time, beating well between additions, to make a dough / Season with salt and black pepper / Place the dough on a floured work surface and roll to 2cm (¾ inch) thick / To make the gnocchi, cut the dough into small pieces and squash lightly with a fork, making an indentation on the top / Bring a pan of salted water to the boil, drop in the gnocchi and bring back to the boil / When the gnocchi rise to the surface, cook for a further 3 minutes / Drain and refresh in iced water if not using immediately.

Sauce
Heat a frying pan, add half the olive oil and the gnocchi and fry until just golden – about 2 minutes / Add the girolles, thyme and some salt and black pepper and fry for 1 minute / Add the shallots and cook for 2–3 minutes / Add the stock and butter and cook for a further 1–2 minutes / Meanwhile, heat a frying pan, add the remaining olive oil and the duck eggs and fry until crisp underneath and soft on top.

To serve
Spoon the gnocchi and sauce into serving bowls / Top each one with a duck egg and grate a few hazelnuts over the top / Finish with parsley shoots and shavings of Parmesan.

Wine expert Susy Atkins's choice
Leyda Pinot Noir Las Brisas
This wine is wonderfully aromatic, with strawberries and cassis just jumping out of the glass. The grape variety is famous for its smooth, rounded texture, and this quality goes really well with this dish.

James Martin
Pumpkin and amaretti tortellini with tomato and basil sauce

The amaretti helps bring out the natural sweetness in the pumpkin. This is a classic Italian combination, normally served in ravioli but equally great in tortellini.

Ingredients Serves 4

Tortellini

250g (9oz) 'OO' pasta flour
3 egg yolks
3 eggs
4 tablespoons olive oil
1.7kg (3lb 1oz) pumpkin, peeled, deseeded and cut into chunks
5 amaretti biscuits, crushed
1 teaspoon lemon juice
½ teaspoon ground ginger

Sauce

4 tablespoons extra virgin olive oil
8 tomatoes, peeled, deseeded and chopped
Large handful of basil leaves

Method

Tortellini

Place the flour in a bowl and season with a little salt and black pepper / Beat the yolks and eggs together in a small bowl / Pour the eggs into the flour and stir until combined to form a stiff dough / Add 2 tablespoons of olive oil at the end, a teaspoon at a time, until the dough is pliable / Place on a lightly floured work surface and knead until the dough is smooth and elastic / Cover with clingfilm and set aside to rest in the fridge for 30 minutes / Roll the dough out in a pasta machine to 1–2 mm thickness and cut into 10cm (4 inch) circles / Meanwhile, preheat the oven to 220°C/425°F/Gas 7 / Toss the pumpkin with salt, black pepper and the remaining 2 tablespoons of olive oil and place on a roasting tray / Place in the oven and roast for 20 minutes until tender / Put the roasted pumpkin into a food processor and blend to a purée / Spoon into a saucepan and place over the heat to drive off any excess moisture, then set aside to cool / When cool, add the amaretti biscuits, lemon juice and ground ginger and check the seasoning / Take a spoonful of the mixture and place in the centre of one of the pasta circles / Brush the edge of the pasta with water / Fold the pasta over to form a half circle, pressing down around the filling to create a seal / Holding each end of the pasta, twist to form a little shell-like shape / Place on a tray lined with baking parchment / Repeat with the remaining filling and pasta.

Sauce

When you have made your tortellini, heat a frying pan and add the olive oil and tomatoes / Cook for 3–4 minutes, until the tomatoes are just starting to break down / Roughly chop the basil, toss into the sauce and season with salt and black pepper.

To serve

Heat a large saucepan of water until boiling and add a pinch of salt / Add the tortellini a few at a time and cook until they float back to the surface, about 1–2 minutes / Drain, then drop the tortellini into the tomato sauce and toss to coat.

Michel Roux
**Apple and passion
fruit tartlets**

James Martin
**Lemon curd meringue tarts
with blackberry compote**

James Martin
**Orange tart with caramelised
oranges and goat's cheese
cream**

James Martin
**Cardamom and coffee cake
with pistachio cream**

James Martin
**Coffee crème brûlée with
fig and pistachio biscotti**

James Martin
**Blueberry clafoutis with
roasted apples**

James Martin
**Dark chocolate tart with
chocolate Turkish delight**

James Martin
**Walnut Bakewell tart
with roasted medlars**

James Martin
**Lardy cake with black
pepper strawberry jam**

Matt Tebbutt
Monmouth pudding

James Martin
**Apple and thyme crumble
with thyme custard**

James Martin
**South American churros
with hot chilli chocolate**

Nick Nairn
**Shirley Spear's marmalade
pudding with Drambuie
custard**

Desserts

Michel Roux
Apple and passion fruit tartlets

Michel began his career as a pastry chef and since then has had a life long passion for pastry. His expert instruction will guarantee you superb results.

Ingredients Serves 6

Rough puff pastry
250g (9oz) plain flour
250g (9oz) very cold butter,
    cut into small cubes
½ teaspoon salt
125ml (4½fl oz) ice-cold water

Crème patissière
3 egg yolks
60g (2½oz) caster sugar
20g (¾oz) plain flour
250ml (9fl oz) milk
½ vanilla pod, split
    lengthways
1 tablespoon icing sugar

Tartlets
3 medium Cox's apples,
    peeled and thinly sliced
60g (2½oz) caster sugar

To serve
3 passion fruits

Method

Rough puff pastry
Put the flour in a mound on a work surface and make a well / Place the butter and salt in the well and work together with your fingertips / When the dough resembles breadcrumbs, gradually add the iced water, mixing until it is all incorporated, but don't overwork it / Roll it into a ball, wrap in clingfilm and refrigerate for 20 minutes / Flour a work surface and roll out the pastry into a 40 x 20cm rectangle, then fold it into three and give it a quarter-turn / Roll the block of pastry into a 40 x 20cm rectangle as before, and fold it into three again / Wrap the block in clingfilm and refrigerate it for 30 minutes / Give the chilled pastry another 2 turns, rolling and folding as before / Wrap it in clingfilm and refrigerate for at least 30 minutes before using.

Crème patissière
Whisk the egg yolks and one-third of the sugar together in a bowl to a light ribbon consistency / Whisk in the flour thoroughly / In a saucepan, heat the milk with the rest of the sugar and the vanilla pod, and as soon as it comes to the boil, pour it on to the egg yolk mixture, stirring continously / Mix well, then return the mixture to the pan and bring to the boil over a medium heat, whisking continuously / Let it bubble for 2 minutes, then pour into a bowl / Dust the crème patissière with a veil of icing sugar to prevent a skin forming as it cools / Once cold, it can be kept in the fridge for up to 3 days / Remember to remove the vanilla pod before serving.

Tartlets
Preheat the oven to 180°C/350°F/Gas 4 and take the pastry and crème patissière out of the fridge / On a lightly floured work surface, roll out the pastry to a 3mm (⅛ inch) thickness / Using a pastry cutter, cut out 6 discs / Brush a baking tray with a little cold water and lift the pastry discs on to it with a palette knife / Refrigerate for 20 minutes, then prick the pastry discs in 5 places with a fork / Divide the crème patissière between them and spread it evenly, leaving a narrow margin around the edge / Arrange the sliced apple over the crème patissière on each disc, radiating from the centre / Bake for 15 minutes, then sprinkle generously with the caster sugar and cook for another 5 minutes / Take the tartlets out of the oven and immediately lift them on to a wire rack with a palette knife.

To serve

Halve the passion fruit and scrape out the pulp and seeds over the tartlets.

Wine expert Susie Barrie's choice
Feiler-Artinger Beerenauslese

James Martin
Lemon curd meringue tarts with blackberry compote

As an alternative to lemon curd you could try making this dish with orange or grapefruit curd, but whatever flavour you choose you'll love it!

Ingredients Serves 4

Tarts
Zest and juice of 4 lemons
4 eggs, beaten
500g (1lb 2oz) caster sugar
110g (4oz) butter
300g (11oz) sweet pastry,
   rolled to 3mm (⅛ inch)
   thick
2 egg whites

Compote
75g (3oz) caster sugar
50ml (2fl oz) crème de mure
250g (9oz) blackberries

To serve

4 sprigs of fresh mint

Method

Tarts
Preheat the oven to 200°C/400°F/Gas 6 / Place the lemon zest and juice, eggs and 350g (12oz) of the sugar into a saucepan and beat well / Place on the heat and bring to a simmer, then add the butter and whisk until combined / Cook for 4–5 minutes, stirring continuously, until thickened, then pour through a fine sieve into a bowl and cool / Line 4 x 10cm (4 inch) diameter shallow tart tins with the pastry and chill for 30 minutes in the fridge / Line with baking parchment and rice or baking beans, and place on a baking tray in the oven for 12 minutes / Remove the baking parchment and rice and return to the oven for 5 minutes / When cooked, remove from the tins and leave to cool slightly, leaving the oven on / Place the remaining 150g (5oz) of caster sugar on a baking tray in the oven for 5 minutes to heat up, but not melt / Place the egg whites in a large bowl and whisk to soft peaks / Gradually add the hot sugar, a third at a time, whisking constantly, until firm peaks form and the meringue turns glossy / Spoon the meringue into a piping bag / Spoon the lemon curd into the cooked pastry cases / Pipe the meringue in concentric circles on top of the lemon curd / Using a blowtorch or grill, glaze the meringue until golden brown.

Compote
While the pastry is in the oven, place the sugar and crème de mure in a small saucepan and bring to a simmer / Cook for 1 minute, then add the blackberries and cook for 2 minutes, until the juice has just thickened and the blackberries are tender.

To serve

Place the tarts on serving plates, spoon the compote alongside and garnish with a sprig of mint.

Wine expert Olly Smith's choice
Two Hands Brilliant Disguise Moscato

James Martin
Orange tart with caramelised oranges and goat's cheese cream

The secret to this recipe is to make a thin pastry without over-rolling. Orange and goat's cheese really work well together.

Ingredients Serves 8

Tart

500g (1lb 2oz) sweet pastry, rolled to 5mm (¼ inch) thick
5 eggs
200g (7oz) caster sugar
250ml (9fl oz) double cream
Zest and juice of 2–3 oranges
– you need 200ml (7fl oz) orange juice

Oranges and cream

4 oranges, peeled and segmented
4 tablespoons caster sugar
110g (4oz) mild goat's cheese
50ml (2fl oz) double cream
2 tablespoons icing sugar

To serve

4 tablespoons icing sugar

Method

Tart

Preheat the oven to 200°C/400°F/Gas 6 / Line a deep 23cm (9 inch) tart tin with the sweet pastry, line with baking parchment and fill with baking beans or rice / Place on a baking tray and bake in the oven for 15 minutes / Remove the baking parchment and baking beans and return to the oven for a further 10 minutes to crisp the base of the tart / Meanwhile place the eggs and sugar in a large bowl and beat until just combined / Add the double cream and orange juice and whisk until fully combined / Pour through a sieve into a jug and add the orange zest / Pour into the pastry case when ready and put back into the oven, turning it down to 130°C/250°F/Gas ½ / Bake for 1–1¼ hours, until just set / Remove from the oven and cool for about 1 hour before removing from the tin.

Oranges and cream

While the tart is cooling, heat a frying pan and add the orange segments / Cook for 1 minute without turning to colour the segments, then turn and cook for a further 30 seconds / Add the sugar and cook until just dissolved / Place the goat's cheese in a bowl, add the cream and icing sugar and beat to a thick cream.

To serve

Dust the tart with the icing sugar and glaze with a blowtorch or under a hot grill until just caramelised / Cut into wedges and place on serving plates / Spoon some hot orange segments alongside and top with a spoonful of goat's cheese cream.

Wine expert Peter Richards's choice
Cantavida Late Harvest

James Martin
Cardamom and coffee cake with pistachio cream

This is a great cake for a school fête, but we think you won't have any left to sell, as it's delicious!

Ingredients Serves 8–10

Cake
200g (7oz) butter
200g (7oz) caster sugar
4 eggs
3 tablespoons strong coffee
8 cardamom pods, split and
    seeds ground
250g (9oz) self-raising flour

Filling
250g (9fl oz) double cream
1 tablespoon icing sugar
5 cardamom pods, split and
    seeds ground
60g (2½oz) pistachios,
    roughly chopped

Icing
110g (4oz) icing sugar
1 tablespoon warm coffee

Method

Cake
Preheat the oven to 190°C/375°F/Gas 5, and butter and line a 23cm (9 inch) deep sandwich tin / Place the butter and sugar in a bowl and beat until light and fluffy / Add the eggs, one at a time, beating in between additions / Add the coffee and ground cardamom and whisk once more / Fold in the flour, making sure it is all incorporated / Pour into the cake tin and place in the oven for 20–25 minutes, until golden and well risen / Remove from the oven and carefully hold level at waist height / Drop it to the floor, taking care to keep the cake in the tin (this releases any trapped air that could cause the cake to sink) / Set aside to cool.

Filling
When the cake has cooled, put the cream into a bowl and whisk to soft peaks / Add the icing sugar, ground cardamom and pistachios and whisk once more to firm peaks.

Icing
Meanwhile place the icing sugar in a bowl, add the coffee and whisk until smooth.

To serve

Cut the cake in half horizontally and place the bottom half on a plate / Spread the pistachio cream over the sponge / Top with the top half of the sponge / Spoon the icing over, allowing it to drizzle down the sides.

James Martin
Coffee crème brûlée with fig and pistachio biscotti

You can flavour crème brûlée with lots of different ingredients. Once you've tried coffee, why not experiment with citrus fruits?

Ingredients Serves 4–6

Brûlée

250ml (9fl oz) full-fat milk
3 tablespoons instant coffee granules
10 egg yolks
175g (6oz) caster sugar
750ml (1 pint 5fl oz) double cream
50g (2oz) demerara sugar

Biscotti

250g (9oz) plain flour
250g (9oz) caster sugar
½ tablespoon baking powder
3 eggs, lightly beaten
225g (8oz) shelled pistachios
125g (4½oz) dried figs, roughly chopped
Zest of 1 lemon

To serve

75ml (3fl oz) whipping cream, lightly whipped
2 tablespoons cocoa powder

Method

Brûlée

Preheat the oven to 130°C/250°F/Gas ½ / Heat the milk in a saucepan, then whisk in the coffee granules until dissolved / Place the egg yolks in a bowl, add the caster sugar and whisk until combined / Add the milk and cream and whisk well / Ladle the mixture into small ramekins, place them in a roasting tin half filled with water, and put in the oven for 1½–2 hours, until set / Cool, then place in the fridge until chilled / When ready to eat, sprinkle the demerara sugar over the top and caramelise with a blowtorch or under the grill.

Biscotti

Preheat the oven to 180°C/350°F/Gas 4 / Mix the flour, sugar and baking powder in a bowl / Add half the beaten eggs and mix well / Add the remaining eggs a little at a time, until the dough takes shape / Add the pistachios, figs and lemon zest and mix to a soft dough / Divide the dough into 6 and roll each piece into a sausage 2.5cm in diameter / Place them at least 6cm (2½ inches) apart on a baking tray and flatten them slightly, then place in the oven for 20–30 minutes / Remove and cool for 10 minutes, until the dough just firms up / Turn the oven down to 140°C/275°F/Gas 1 / Using a serrated knife, cut the biscotti on an angle into 5mm (¼ inch) slices / Place back on the baking tray, and return it to the oven for 12 minutes / Turn the biscotti over and bake for a further 10–15 minutes, until they are golden / Remove from the oven and cool totally before storing.

To serve

Place a ramekin on each serving plate and top the brûlée with a dollop of whipped cream / Dust lightly with cocoa powder and serve with the biscotti.

Wine expert Olly Smith's choice
Tesco Finest Botrytis Semillon

James Martin
Blueberry clafoutis with roasted apples

This traditional French cake is usually made with black cherries, but it's also delicious with blueberries.

Ingredients Serves 4–6

Clafoutis
125ml (4½fl oz) full-fat milk
125ml (4½fl oz) double cream
½ vanilla pod, split and
    scraped
4 eggs
175g (6oz) caster sugar
75g (3oz) plain flour
1 tablespoon crème de cassis
500g (1Ib 2oz) blueberries
2 tablespoons icing sugar

Apples
50g (2oz) butter
50g (2oz) caster sugar
2 Cox's apples, peeled and cut
    into wedges
175g (6oz) blueberries

Sauce
50g (2oz) caster sugar
50ml (2fl oz) crème de cassis
150g (5oz) blueberries

To serve
150g (5oz) clotted cream

Method

Clafoutis
Preheat the oven to 190°C/375°F/Gas 5 / Combine the milk, cream and vanilla pod in a saucepan over a medium heat and boil for 1 minute / In a bowl, whisk the eggs and sugar until light and frothy / Add the flour / Discard the vanilla pod and pour the milk mixture on to the eggs, whisking lightly / Stir in the crème de cassis and leave the mixture in a cool place, stirring from time to time / Arrange three-quarters of the blueberries in an ovenproof dish, pour over the egg mixture and scatter the remaining blueberries over the top / Bake for 40–45 minutes, until the pudding just wobbles when shaken lightly / Remove and dust with icing sugar.

Apples
When the clafoutis is nearly ready, heat a frying pan, add the butter and sugar and cook for 1 minute until lightly caramelised / Add the apples and sauté for 2–3 minutes, until golden and tender / Add the blueberries, toss together and cook for 1 more minute.

Sauce
While the apples are cooking, place the sugar and crème de cassis in a small saucepan and bring to the boil / Simmer for 2 minutes, then add the blueberries and cook for 1 minute / Pour into a blender and blitz to a purée / Pass through a sieve back into a saucepan and cook for 1 minute.

To serve
Place a spoonful of sauce in the centre of each serving plate / Top with a spoonful of clafoutis and pile some apples and blueberries alongside / Serve with clotted cream.

Wine expert Susie Barrie's choice
Almond Grove Noble Late Harvest Riesling

James Martin
Dark chocolate tart with chocolate Turkish delight

Make sure you use non-stick baking parchment, otherwise the Turkish delight won't lift off the tray.

Ingredients Serves 6–8

Turkish delight
450g (1lb) granulated sugar
Juice of 1 lemon
600ml (1 pint) water
75g (3oz) cornflour
1 teaspoon cream of tartar
3 tablespoons rose water
3 tablespoons icing sugar
110g (4oz) dark chocolate
    (85% cocoa solids), melted

Tart
375g (13oz) sweet pastry
400g (14oz) dark chocolate
    (85% cocoa solids), roughly
    chopped
250ml (10fl oz) double cream
2 egg yolks

To serve

1 tub of vanilla ice cream

Method

Turkish delight
Line a 23cm (9 inch) square baking tray with non-stick baking parchment / Place the sugar, lemon juice and 200ml (7fl oz) of the water in a saucepan / Place on the heat and bring to the boil, and cook until the temperature reaches 240°C on a sugar thermometer / Meanwhile, place the cornflour, cream of tartar and remaining water in a saucepan and whisk together, then place on the heat and cook until thickened / When the sugar reaches 240°C, pour in the cornflour mixture and whisk vigorously to combine / Return to the heat and cook over a low heat for 20–30 minutes, until thickened and a lightly golden brown colour / Remove from the heat, add the rose water and beat well / Pour into the prepared baking tray and smooth to the edges / Place in the fridge for at least 1 hour, until chilled and set / Dust a piece of non-stick baking parchment with icing sugar, turn out the Turkish delight on to the paper, and cut it into squares / Dust one-third of them in icing sugar and set aside / Dip the remaining squares into the melted chocolate and place on a plate in the fridge to set.

Tart
While the Turkish delight is setting in the fridge, preheat the oven to 180°C/350°F/Gas 4 and butter a 20cm (8 inch) loose-bottomed tart tin / On a lightly floured surface, roll out the pastry and use to line the tin, then cover and place in the fridge for 30 minutes / Line the pastry case with baking parchment, fill with baking beans and bake in the oven for 10–15 minutes / Remove the baking parchment and beans, and return the tart case to the oven for a further 3–5 minutes, until it is just cooked / Reduce the heat to 170°C/325°F/Gas 3 / Meanwhile, put the chocolate and cream into a bowl and place over a pan of boiling water / Heat until the chocolate has melted, then remove from the heat and whisk the egg yolks into the mixture / Spoon into the pastry case, smoothing to the edges, and put in the oven for 15 minutes, until just set / Remove from the oven and allow to cool to room temperature before serving.

To serve

Put a slice of the tart in the centre of each serving plate / Place 2 pieces of chocolate and 1 of plain Turkish delight alongside, and finish with a spoonful of ice cream.

Wine expert Olly Smith's choice
Nyetimber Cuvée Classic

James Martin
Walnut Bakewell tart with roasted medlars

The medlar is a cousin of the apple and also makes a wonderful compote or jelly.

Ingredients Serves 10–12

Tart
500g (1Ib 2oz) sweet pastry, rolled to 5mm (¼ inch) thick
175g (6oz) butter
175g (6oz) caster sugar
4 eggs
175g (6oz) ground walnuts
110g (4oz) breadcrumbs
200g (7oz) damson jam
12 walnut halves

Medlars
50g (2oz) butter
400g (14oz) medlars
75g (3oz) caster sugar
1 cinnamon stick

Damson cream
250ml (9fl oz) double cream
110g (4oz) damson jam

Method

Tart
Preheat the oven to 190°C/375°F/Gas 5 / Line a deep 23cm (9 inch) tart tin with the sweet pastry, line with clingfilm and fill with baking beans or rice / Place on a baking tray and put in the oven for 15 minutes / Remove the clingfilm and baking beans and bake for a further 10 minutes to crisp the base of the tart / Place the butter and sugar in a bowl and beat until light and fluffy / Add the eggs and beat once more / Add the ground walnuts and breadcrumbs and fold in thoroughly / Spoon the damson jam across the bottom of the tart / Cover with the walnut filling and smooth the top / Carefully arrange the walnut halves around the edge of the filling / Place in the oven for 25–30 minutes, until risen and golden brown / Remove from the oven and set aside to cool slightly.

Medlars
While the tart is cooling, increase the oven temperature to 200°C/400°F/Gas 6 / Heat an ovenproof frying pan, then add the butter and medlars and sauté for 1–2 minutes / Add the sugar and cinnamon and place in the oven for 10–15 minutes, until the medlars are soft and the skins have split.

Damson cream
While the medlars are cooking, whip the cream until soft peaks are formed, then fold in the damson jam.

To serve

Place a slice of tart in the centre of each serving plate and top with a spoonful of damson cream / Place a couple of medlars to the side.

Wine expert Olly Smith's choice
Domaine des Forges, Chaume 1er Cru Coteaux du Layon

James Martin
Lardy cake with black pepper strawberry jam

Using lard may be unfashionable now but it makes this traditional cake delicious, and it shouldn't be a forgotten ingredient.

Ingredients Serves 4–6

Cake

225g (8oz) sultanas
90g (3½oz) lard, plus
  1 tablespoon extra for
  greasing
125g (4½oz) light muscovado
  sugar
2 tablespoons golden syrup
225ml (8fl oz) water
225g (8oz) wholemeal flour
1 teaspoon baking powder
½ teaspoon bicarbonate of
  soda
¼ teaspoon ground nutmeg
1 teaspoon ground allspice
4 eggs, lightly beaten

Jam

600g (1lb 5oz) jam sugar
Zest and juice of 1 lemon
1kg (2lb 2oz) strawberries,
  whole
1 teaspoon crushed black
  peppercorns

Method

Cake

Preheat the oven to 180°C/350°F/Gas 4, and grease and line a small loaf tin / Place the sultanas, lard, sugar, golden syrup and water in a saucepan and bring to the boil, stirring continuously / Remove from the heat and cool / Sift the flour, baking powder, bicarbonate of soda and spices into a large bowl / Mix the cooled sultana mixture into the dried ingredients along with the eggs, beating well to combine / Tip the cake mixture into the cake tin and level the top / Place in the oven for 1–1¼ hours, until the top is golden brown and a skewer comes out clean / Cool in the tin for 30 minutes, then turn out and cool completely on a wire rack.

Jam

While the cake is cooking, place the sugar, lemon zest and juice in a large pan and heat until the sugar has dissolved / Add the strawberries and black pepper, bring to the boil and cook for 5 minutes / Leave to cool, then skim off any froth and spoon into sterilised jars.

To serve

Slice the cake and spread generously with the jam.

Matt Tebbutt
Monmouth pudding

This recipe originates from near Matt's home in South Wales. It also works well with rhubarb.

Ingredients Serves 4–6

Base and filling
90g (3½oz) fresh breadcrumbs
2 tablespoons soft light brown sugar
450ml (16fl oz) milk
Zest of 1 lemon
2 tablespoons caster sugar
25g (1oz) salted butter
3 large egg yolks
150g (5oz) frozen raspberries
175g (6oz) raspberry jam, preferably homemade

Meringue
3 large egg whites
75g (3oz) caster sugar

Method

Base and filling
Heat the grill to medium / Place the breadcrumbs on a tray and sprinkle with the soft brown sugar / Toss to combine, then place under the grill and cook until lightly toasted / Remove and set aside / Preheat the oven to 150°C/300°F/Gas 2 / Put the milk, lemon zest, caster sugar and butter into a saucepan and place on the heat / Cook until the butter has melted, then stir in the toasted breadcrumbs and leave to stand for 30 minutes / Beat the egg yolks into the breadcrumb mixture, then pour into a 20cm (8 inch) ovenproof serving dish / Place in the oven and bake for 25–30 minutes, until just set / Remove from the oven and increase the temperature to 180°C/350°F/Gas 4 / Scatter the raspberries over the top of the dish and spoon the jam over.

Meringue
Place the egg whites in a bowl and whisk until they form firm peaks / Add the sugar and whisk again until stiff / Spoon the meringue over the dish and put back into the oven for 8–10 minutes, until golden / Serve warm.

Wine expert Peter Richards's choice
Moscato Freisa Vino Spumante
When matching wine to puddings you should consider the dominant flavour, and in this dish it is raspberries, so we need a wine that's not too heavy or honeyed. This sparkling wine is full of fruit, which will refresh the palate between mouthfuls.

James Martin
Apple and thyme crumble with thyme custard

Using thyme in this recipe brings an exciting twist to the 'humble' crumble.

Ingredients Serves 6

Crumble
200g (7oz) butter
1.5kg (3lb 4oz) Bramley apples, peeled and cut into chunks
150g (5oz) caster sugar, plus 4 tablespoons
6 sprigs of fresh lemon thyme, leaves picked
300g (11oz) plain flour

Custard
200ml (7fl oz) milk
200ml (7fl oz) double cream
4 sprigs of fresh thyme, leaves picked
6 egg yolks
75g (3oz) caster sugar

Method

Crumble
Preheat the oven to 200°C/400°F/Gas 6 / Heat a saucepan, add the 50g (2oz) of the butter, the apples, the 4 tablespoons of sugar and thyme, and cook for 5–8 minutes until the apples are soft / Pour them into a greased baking dish / Mix the remaining butter and flour together until the mixture resembles breadcrumbs / Add the remaining 150g (6oz) of sugar and mix well / Spoon the crumble over the top of the apples / Place in the oven for 15–20 minutes, until golden and bubbling.

Custard
When the crumble is nearly ready, place the milk and cream in a saucepan over a low heat, add the thyme and simmer very gently for 5 minutes to infuse the flavour / Beat together the egg yolks and sugar in a bowl / Pour the hot milk on to the eggs and stir well, then return to the pan and cook until just thickened.

To serve

Place a spoonful of crumble on each serving plate and top with the thyme custard.

Wine expert Susy Atkins's choice
Moscatel de Valencia

James Martin
South American churros with hot chilli chocolate

Churros are a type of Spanish doughnut that are sold freshly made and piping hot on the streets of Mexico and Argentina.

Ingredients Serves 4

Churros
250ml (9fl oz) water
75g (3oz) butter
200g (7oz) plain flour
¼ teaspoon baking powder
1 egg, beaten
60g (2½oz) caster sugar
½ teaspoon ground cinnamon

Hot chilli chocolate
500ml (18fl oz) full-fat milk
160g (5½oz) dark chocolate
   (70%), finely chopped
½ –1 teaspoon chilli powder
2 teaspoons caster sugar

Method

Churros
Heat a deep-fat fryer to 130°C / Place the water in a saucepan with the butter / Place on the heat and bring to the boil / When boiling, add the flour and baking powder and beat to a smooth batter / Remove from the heat and beat in the egg, continuing to beat until the batter is smooth and shiny / Place a large star nozzle in a piping bag and fill with the batter / Pipe directly into the deep-fat fryer – in lines or circles or spirals / Cook for 2–3 minutes, until golden and crispy / Remove from the oil to a plate lined with kitchen paper / Toss the sugar and ground cinnamon together on a plate / Add the churros and carefully roll in the sugar mix.

Hot chilli chocolate
When the churros are ready, make the hot chilli chocolate / Place the milk in a saucepan and bring to the boil / Remove from the heat, add the chocolate, chilli powder and sugar and whisk vigorously until the chocolate is melted and the mixture frothy / Return to the heat for 1 minute.

To serve

Serve the churros as soon as they are ready, with mugs or cups of the hot chilli chocolate.

Nick Nairn
Shirley Spear's marmalade pudding with Drambuie custard

This is a great alternative to Christmas pudding, but wonderful after any meal. Using breadcrumbs makes it nice and light.

Ingredients Serves 6

Pudding

150g (5oz) fine brown
  breadcrumbs
125g (4½oz) soft light brown
  sugar
25g (1oz) self-raising
  wholemeal flour
125g (4½oz) butter, plus extra
  for greasing the bowl
175g (6oz) well-flavoured
  coarse-cut marmalade
3 large eggs
1 rounded teaspoon
  bicarbonate of soda
1 tablespoon cold water

Drambuie custard

1 vanilla pod
300ml (11fl oz) double cream
300ml (11fl oz) milk
6 egg yolks
50g (2oz) caster sugar
2–3 tablespoons Drambuie

To serve

5 tablespoons well-flavoured
  coarse-cut marmalade

Method

Pudding

Butter a 1.5 litre (3 pint) pudding basin (or heatproof plastic basin with matching lid) / Place the breadcrumbs, sugar and flour in a large mixing bowl / Melt the butter with the marmalade in a saucepan over a gentle heat, but do not boil / Pour the melted ingredients into the breadcrumb mixture and mix together thoroughly / Break the eggs in to a bowl and whisk until frothy, then beat gently into the mixture until well blended / Dissolve the bicarbonate of soda in the cold water / Beat this into the pudding mixture, which will increase in volume as it absorbs the bicarbonate of soda / Transfer the mixture to the prepared pudding basin and leave to stand for 5 minutes for the bicarbonate to work / Cover the basin with baking parchment then foil and secure tightly (or cover with a close-fitting heatproof lid) / Place it in a saucepan of boiling water – the water should reach halfway up the side / Simmer the pudding steadily for 2 hours – the water will need topping up throughout the cooking period.

Drambuie custard

When the pudding is ready, split open the vanilla pod and scrape out the seeds into a pan / Add the cream, milk and vanilla pod and slowly bring to the boil / Put the egg yolks and caster sugar into a bowl and beat until pale and creamy / Pour the boiled cream over the egg yolks, stirring all the time / Pour back into the pan, add the Drambuie and place over a very low heat, stirring with a wooden spoon for 2–3 minutes until it begins to thicken (don't let it get too hot, or it may curdle).

To serve

Uncover the pudding and turn it out on to a warmed serving dish / Melt the marmalade and drizzle over the pudding before serving / Cut into wedges and serve with the Drambuie custard.

Wine expert Olly Smith's choice
Campbell's Rutherglen Muscat
This wine's been fortified and that keeps the sweetness and intensifies the flavours. If you give it a sniff there's a world of dried fruit, perfect for this pud!

Index

Index